# GOETHE'S THEORY OF KNOWLEDGE

RUDOLF STEINER (1885)

# GOETHE'S THEORY OF KNOWLEDGE

## An Outline of the Epistemology of His Worldview

Written 1884-1885
First Published 1886

TRANSLATED BY PETER CLEMM
INTRODUCTION BY CHRISTOPHER BAMFORD

RUDOLF STEINER

SteinerBooks

CW 2

SteinerBooks
Anthroposophic Press
610 Main Street
Great Barrington, Massachusetts 01230
www.steinerbooks.org

Translation from the German by Peter Clemm

This book is volume 2 in the Collected Works (CW) of Rudolf Steiner, published by SteinerBooks, 2008. It is a translation of *Grundlinien einer Erkenntnistheorie der Goetheschen Weltanschauung*, published by Rudolf Steiner Verlag, Dornach, Switzerland, 2003. It was first published in German in 1886.

Library of Congress Cataloging-in-Publication Data

Steiner, Rudolf, 1861-1925.
[Grundlinien einer Erkenntnistheorie der Goetheschen Weltanschauung. English]
Goethe's theory of knowledge : an outline of the epistemology of his worldview, written 1884-1885 / translated by Peter Clemm ; introduction by Christopher Bam ford ; Rudolf Steiner. — 1st ed.
p. cm. — (Collected Works of Rudolf Steiner ; v. 2)
First published: Dornach, Swizerland : Rudolf Steiner, 1886.
ISBN 978-0-88010-623-8
1. Goethe, Johann Wolfgang von, 1749-1832—Philosophy. 2. Knowledge, Theory of. I. Title.
PT2193.S83213 2008
831'.6–dc22
2008017137



Printed in the United States

# CONTENTS

D. Knowledge



E. Knowing Nature



F. The Humanities



G. Conclusion

# INTRODUCTION

## Christopher Bamford

We often forget both how brilliant the young Rudolf Steiner was, and, though evolving in his conceptions, how consistent and undeviating the course of his thinking remained throughout his life. Rarely in cultural history—certain saints excepted—do we find a philosopher or spiritual teacher who demonstrates so determined a single-mindedness, and so evident a grasp of destiny, at so early an age. But such is the case with Rudolf Steiner, who wrote the present book, which is as relevant today as when he wrote it more than a hundred years ago when he was between the ages of twenty-three and twenty-four.

Preceded into print only by the first introductions to the Kürschner edition of Goethe's scientific writings and the short essays ("Atomism" and "Nature and Our Ideals"), *Goethe's Theory of Knowledge* was Steiner's first book.* It is a remarkable performance, communicating the white heat, passion, and intensity of thinking that only youth's vitality can summon. "One can write in such a seminal way only at the beginning of one's path of knowledge," as he says. Reintroducing it forty years later, he could say with confidence that "as a theory of knowledge it seems to form the justification for everything I have said and published since then." In other words, by means of the path of thinking laid down here, Steiner began the process of breaking the ground in which, the seeds of spiritual science, which he would be called upon to inaugurate, could germinate.

Opening a cognitive path from the sensory world to the spiritual world, *Goethe's Theory of Knowledge* thus forms the necessary prologue to a full understanding not only of Steiner's subsequent "epistemological" (or philosophical) works, like *Truth and Knowledge* and *The Philosophy of Freedom*, but also of Anthroposophy as such. The book is often overlooked, however, either because, as he says, "it bears the marks of a kind of thinking prevalent at the time," or because it is mistakenly thought of as being about Goethe's, rather than Steiner's, theory of knowledge. Nevertheless, it is in fact one of Rudolf Steiner's most seminal works.

To appreciate it, however, some understanding of its background is necessary, for as Steiner admits, "it bears the marks of its time."

And so, with perfect spiritual timing, we begin in October 1879, when, synchronously with what he would later call the beginning of the "Michael Age," Rudolf Steiner entered the Technical College in Vienna. He was eighteen-and-a-half, and on a scholarship. A science major, he took as his required courses mathematics, physics, botany, zoology, and chemistry, receiving the grade of "excellent" in all subjects. He also sat in on many other courses, above all in literature and philosophy.

Already, then, he was a "Renaissance man," with wide interests and a deep devotion to truth, however and wherever he could find it. Yet, though avowedly bookish, he was no cloistered, ivory tower scholar. Intensely social, he always enjoyed a wide range of acquaintances and friends, and was not averse to frequenting coffee houses and nighttime haunts, or to appreciating the warmth and conviviality (the Viennese "*Gemütlichkeit*") of the conversations that took place there.

Philosophy was particularly important to him. In fact, it was his passion. He had been studying Kant since he was sixteen and since then had continued to read widely and deeply in German idealism (above all, Fichte, Hegel, and Schelling), as well as in the contemporary philosophical—mostly neo-Kantian—literature of his time. Kant's "Copernican revolution" had reduced the human capacity to know to the reasoning mind. For Kant, that mind alone was the source of knowledge. Essentially, according to him, we could know only our own "a priori" forms of knowing. Indeed, as Otto Liebmann, one of the Neo-Kantians, elaborated: human consciousness could know only itself. Other contemporary philosophers Steiner read, like Johannes Volkelt and Edouard von Hartmann, agreed: "Reality" was a closed book, unknowable and unknown. However much human beings could know, they would be limited to—that is, starkly stated, imprisoned by—their mental pictures or representations. Consciousness was not universal. It had no larger, unifying reality, but was essentially an impermeable barrier shutting off the world, which in its own reality was thus condemned to remain forever unknown. The phenomena of nature—"things in themselves"—and spiritual, non-mental realities were intrinsically unknowable. Consciousness was restricted to the purely mental, and hence the world was reduced to a simulacrum.

Because he knew from his own experience that the truth was otherwise, Steiner from the beginning sought a non-reductive epistemology, one founded in the wholeness of the spirit and of the human person: the unity of consciousness and cosmos. Without such an epistemology, science in the sense of true knowledge was impossible. It remained a merely abstract construct; not truly abstract like mathematics, which had its own reality, but rather a kind of abstract figment: not really true either to the physical or the spiritual world.

Thus, from his earliest years, Rudolf Steiner's project was to create a holistic philosophical path of knowledge. He wanted to establish a continuous epistemological bridge that could unite the cognitive world of the thinking mind with both the physical, perceptual realm and the suprasensory realms—realms which, again on the basis of his own clairvoyant experiences, he knew to be true and to possess another, higher, order of reality (and thinking). As he writes in his *Autobiography*: "My task was to study mathematics and natural science. I was convinced, however, that I would find no relation to these sciences unless their results rested on a secure philosophical foundation."

In his first semester, he already attended courses by the important and influential philosopher Franz Brentano, whose other students included Edmund Husserl (founder of phenomenology), T.G. Masarik (founder of modern Czechoslovakia, now the Czech Republic), and even Sigmund Freud (founder of psychoanalysis). An essentially spiritual man, and a Roman Catholic, Brentano studied the relations between what he called sensory and "noetic" consciousness. This was precisely Steiner's field of interest. Best known for the reintroduction of the concepts of intentionality, interiority, and experience to any study of human knowing and being, Brentano sought to create a "scientific psychology" or "science of mental phenomena." Extraordinarily rigorous and logical (and also spiritual) in his thinking, Brentano's vision of philosophy coincided at many levels with Steiner's, holding, for example, that philosophy should become the method of natural science. Brentano's historical impact was enormous and widespread, and not only through his immediate students. His doctoral dissertation *On the Several Senses of Being in Aristotle*, for example, was a primary influence on Martin Heidegger's recovery of ontology in *Being and Time*, which was of course dependent for its phenomenology on Husserl, Brentano's prize disciple. Brentano was also clearly influential on Rudolf Steiner's own formation, though this has not yet been studied in any detail. As Steiner himself says, after describing attending his lectures, "The stimulus of Brentano had strong, lasting effects on me. I soon began to study his writings, and during later years I have read most of what he has published." Steiner's last "philosophical" work, *The Riddles of the Soul* (CW 21), written 1916-17, in fact contains a homage and "farewell" to Brentano, who had just died. Steiner also studied with the now-forgotten neo-Kantian (so-called "Herbartian") Robert Zimmerman, who also had his influence. It was in one of Zimmerman's works that Steiner would later find the term "anthroposophy," although Zimmerman was by no means the first person to use it. Not surprisingly, too, in search of grist for his philosophical mill, Steiner spent whatever spare time he had in the library. He was determined to leave no page unturned, if some instinct or barely noticed footnote suggested it might be relevant.

Almost immediately upon entering the university, as if there was no time to lose, Steiner's destiny took hold of him. Thus, during that first winter semester, he also first encountered the writer, educator, philologist, Goethe scholar, and historian of literature, Karl Julius Schröer, whom Steiner called "the living embodiment of German education at its best." Steiner took Schröer's course in German Literature, "Schiller's Life and Work," following it in spring with a second course, "Poetry since Goethe." Study of Goethe and Schiller seemed to leaven that of philosophy, and the combination provided a fully human ballast with which to try to understand the basis of the sciences. Again, his grades were "excellent." Probably more important at this stage than anything he learned, however, was the personal (or "karmic") connection with Schröer, who "first became my teacher, and then an older friend." In a very short time, the friendship with Schröer would lead Steiner to the assignment to work as the editor of Goethe's scientific writings: a task that took more than a decade and would change the editor forever.

At another level, Schröer's confirmed idealism, and particularly his understanding of the special nature of German idealism, would naturally have been well received by Steiner. He pays homage to Schröer in *The Riddle of Humanity* (CW 20), quoting from his old teacher's then controversial book, *German Poetry of the Nineteenth Century*:

> The world-rejuvenating appearance of idealism a hundred years ago in Germany in an age of frivolity is the greatest phenomenon of modern history. Both the intellect that is focused only on what is finite and never penetrating to the depths of essential being, and the egotism that is focused only on satisfying sensual needs, retreated before the appearance of a spirit that rose above everything common.

As for the nature of this idealism, exemplified by Goethe and his Faust, Schröer writes:

> Within what is perceived experientially—hidden behind what is finite, behind what can be known by experience—determining factors are everywhere recognizable. These factors must be called the *undetermined* and must be sensed everywhere to be what is constant in change, an eternal lawfulness, and something infinite. The perceived infinite within the finite appears as "idea," and the ability to perceive the infinite appears as "reason," in contrast to "intellect" which remains stuck at what is finite and can perceive nothing beyond it.

Steiner would never become an "idealist" in Schröer's sense, but he would absorb his idealism and transform it.

That summer of 1880, "through a remarkable chain of circumstances," Steiner also met another significant teacher, but this time not one attached to the university. Felix Kogutski (1833-1909) was "a simple man of the people"—a factory worker, herb-gatherer, naturopath—and a mystic. They met on the train to Vienna. Steiner was going to school; Kogutski was traveling to the city to sell his medicinal herbs to pharmacies. Seeing each other frequently, they became friends. It was another turning point. Here was a realized, grounded mystic, a living Rosicrucian (as it were), who understood the inner worlds of nature—"contact with the spirits of nature was something self-evident to him." With him, Steiner could for the first time speak openly of his spiritual experiences.

As their relationship developed, it became clear that their connection went very deep. "From our first meeting I had a deep affinity with him," Steiner writes. "Gradually it seemed as though I were in the company of a soul from ancient times—one untouched by civilization, science, and modern views—who brought me the natural knowledge of ancient times..." Kogutski, however, although he made a powerful and lasting impression on Steiner (he appears as Felix Balde in his *Mystery Dramas*), and even initiated Steiner in a certain way, was not his initiator. His task was only to lead Steiner to the "Master." Steiner, in his autobiographical notes for Édouard Schuré (the so-called "Barr Document") refers to Kogutski as "the agent of the M. [the Master]," his "emissary." Of this mysterious figure, generally assumed to be Christian Rosenkreutz, little is known. It is even unclear whether Steiner first encountered him in the spirit or the body. One has the sense, however, that the relationship, once initiated, continued in some form or other throughout Steiner's life. In the present context, all that need be said is that the Master reaffirmed what Steiner already seemed to have taken to be his task: namely, to construct a bridge from natural scientific thinking and the world of science to the world of the spirit. He also advised Steiner to study Fichte's philosophical work, for it would be there that he would find his path revealed.

The clue would lead Steiner to the primacy of the "I"—that is, freedom—as the source of any truly inclusive epistemology. Kant, while initiating his revolution, had left open the starting-point or foundation of his philosophy. The absolute ground or principle upon which human experience could be founded still remained to be resolved. Building upon Kant's assertion of the primacy of the cognitive faculty as the key to understanding the human being in the world, Fichte found this starting-point or foundation—"the ground of all experience"—in the "I." In a move foreshadowing Hegelian dialectic, Fichte discovered that self-consciousness depended logically on three propositions: identity, contradiction, and synthesis. He saw that the principle of identity (A=A) was presupposed in every moment of consciousness (I=I). It was a logical "fact," but to become an "act" of consciousness, something must posit it: to become experience, the "I" must be posited. Thus he came to the self-positing "I." In positing itself, however, the "I" also posits an "object," an "other," by definition a "Not-I"—in other words: a contradiction. And yet, at the same time, in the act of self-consciousness, we experience ourselves as identical with our selves. In other words, the synthesis is achieved. Such, for Fichte, is the process of knowing. It rests on the fundamental proposition that "the 'I' posits itself purely and simply." Put this way, Fichte's approach sounds very abstract. But, in fact, Fichte's path is phenomenological and meditative. That, too, would have been a clue.

On a less exalted level, his meeting with Felix Kogutski made Steiner realize more clearly than before that no contemporary philosophy had as yet extended to spiritual perception of the kind that Kogutski and Steiner himself had come to experience. As Steiner meditated on this fact, "a theory of knowledge" began to take shape within him. The act of thinking, as he experienced it, touched and communicated reality in a way that the senses did not. Sensory experience might reveal something real within or behind the sensory world, but thinking experience seemed able somehow to grasp reality directly. At the same time, it was as if what thinking could grasp were precisely what sensory experience concealed. In other words, he recognized that thoughts were precisely what the sensory world used to express its true nature: they were the other side of sensory reality. But he also understood that it was important not to move too quickly from that insight toward the development of his own philosophical point of view. To do so might even be dangerous. Such things must develop slowly and organically, even if this sometimes seemed counterproductive.

In this spirit, Steiner began an intense study of Hegel, who clearly grasped the reality of thinking and consciousness. Unfortunately, and tragically, however, Hegel remained at the level of dialectical consciousness—or dialectical thinking—and was unable to penetrate to the "concrete world of the spirit" to which his path might have led. Nevertheless, Steiner found his insights into the living processes of thinking to be invaluable.

Meanwhile there was much to glean, too, from his required courses. Mathematics, which came naturally to Steiner and in which he was already well advanced, continued to furnish a significant foundation for meditation. There is one set of insights concerning the nature of space and time that he mentions as particularly important. The notion of empty Euclidean space, infinite in all directions, seemed unthinkable. On the other hand, non-Euclidean synthetic projective geometry proposed that any line infinitely extended in one direction would return to its starting point from another. There was closure: "A point infinitely distant to the right is the same as a point infinitely distant to the left," as he puts it. In other words, space is closed. "The idea of a straight line returning to itself like a circle was like a revelation." And what if time was the same? "Could the same ideas be applied here—including the idea that, by continuing into the 'infinite future,' one would return from the past?"

Since Steiner mentions this insight in his *Autobiography*, written at the end of his life, it must have been of great significance. Indeed, it may be related to an enigmatic statement in the opening of the so-called Barr Document, where, after speaking of his involvement in philosophy, Steiner goes on to say—although disclaiming that it had anything to do with his studies, but was "guided totally by the spiritual life"—that, "during this period—and this is already due to external spiritual influences—I gained complete understanding of the concept of time.... I understood that there is a regressive evolution, the astral-occult, which interferes with the progressive one. This knowledge is the precondition of spiritual clairvoyance." We may perhaps also connect this same insight with his later assertion that "everything is a vortex"—a double vortex. That is, every living phenomenon is the polaric conjunction of two streams or forces.

It is clear, then, that Steiner's first years at the Technical College were so full that they would have overwhelmed a lesser person.

Reading his account of them, one has the feeling that he is passing through some kind of spiritual and intellectual crucible. Science, philosophy, and literature: all seemed to converge in him in what he felt to be the necessity of finding a new path, one that would resolve the contradictions implicit in trying to harmonize the then ruling paradigm of mechanist-materialist physics (interpreted according to Neo-Kantian epistemology) with his own spiritual insights, which he had tested and confirmed by his own experience. Organic science, for its part, was then, as it is still now, "permeated with Darwinian concepts." From the point of view that human beings are spiritual beings, the premises underlying these concepts were "scientifically impossible." Steiner knew irrefutably from his own experience that, in their inner nature, human beings are spiritual beings—members, as he puts it, "of the world of spirit"—who, as it were, "dip down" from the spiritual world into physical existence to perceive and act in the sensory world. This view simply could not be reconciled with Darwinism, though it was not antithetical to the idea of evolution. Instead, it placed evolution in a spiritual context: evolution was fundamentally a spiritual evolution; what "evolved" was "spirit," not "matter." Thus Steiner found himself painfully grappling with the horns of an irresolvable dilemma. As he writes in his *Autobiography*: "The idea of higher organisms evolving out of lower ones seemed fruitful to me, but to combine this idea with what I knew as the world of spirit was infinitely difficult."

Similar difficulties arose in physics, when he tried to unite contemporary theories of heat, light, or electricity—all essentially nominalist—with what he felt to be spiritually true and in accord with reality. For science, there was nothing but matter in motion, which was thought mysteriously to give rise to sensations and perceptions in human consciousness. But these had nothing to do with the fundamental reality, which was just matter in motion. Neither sound nor light, for instance, had a universal, concrete reality, distinct from their manifestations in space. For Steiner, in contrast, light seemed to have a universality that was distinct from its manifestation as color in illuminated space. Color, therefore, was a revelation of light which, acting as "an extrasensory reality within the sensory world," both veiled and unveiled it. From this point of view, sense perceptions could unfold into suprasensory realities. And yet, for ordinary science, human sensory perceptions—and the qualities that they provided—were only subjective experiences and nothing more. Spirit was thus driven from the so-called outer world, while the inner world for its part was simply an illusory epiphenomenon of matter. In this way, again and again, Steiner found himself confronted with the "inner agony" that he would find no solution to the question of the relationship between spiritual and sensory realities, unless he could articulate an epistemology or theory of knowing that would demonstrate the continuity between the inner and outer worlds—an epistemology that, as he would later put it, united the spiritual in the human being with the spiritual in the world, for the explanation and understanding of both.

As Steiner wrestled with such problems, he found himself returning again and again to the unitive character of thinking. The poet, philosopher, and dramatist, Friedrich Schiller helped by pointing out that human consciousness, in its relationship with the world, oscillates between different states. For Schiller, the most important was the state between that in which we are surrendered to the senses and that in which we withdraw from sensory reality and live entirely in the world of logic and reason. Schiller called this intermediate state "aesthetic." Through it, we experience beauty. It lives through the senses, but brings something spiritual to them, uniting sense perception with a kind of thinking. In other words, in the experience of beauty we enter a state in which we are united with the world in such a way that allows it to reveal its spiritual nature. Focusing his attention on this state, Steiner began to have an inkling of another reality when he began to understand that the thought-content that unites us with the world in the experience of beauty could be experienced in itself. Experiencing the cognitive reality of beauty, he realized that thinking itself is quite different from having thoughts. Penetrating this experience more deeply, he began to sense how a different kind of thinking—living thinking—could provide a point of entry into the single reality, which ordinary consciousness bifurcates into the subjective and objective worlds; he realized that there was, in fact, an extrasensory reality within the sensory world.

There were other advances, too. The earliest document we have from Steiner's hand is a letter, written to his friend Joseph Kock, on January 13, 1881.

> Dear faithful friend,
> It was the night from January 10th to the 11th. I didn't sleep a wink. I was busy with philosophical problems until about 12.30 a.m., when, finally, I threw myself onto my couch. I had striven the previous year to research whether what Schelling said was true or not: "Within all of us a secret, marvelous capacity dwells whereby we can withdraw from the mutability of time—out of the self clothed in all that comes to us from outside—into our innermost being and there, in the immutable form of the unchanging, behold the eternal in ourselves." I believed then and still believe now that I discovered that inner capacity within myself. I had long had an inkling of it. Now the whole of idealistic philosophy stands before me transformed in its essence. What's a sleepless night compared to that! ...

Clearly, philosophy for the young Rudolf Steiner was not an abstraction, but an experience. It was not something one just thought about; it was an inner activity of the soul. It was something one did. It was, in fact, a way of life: a spiritual path.

In another early letter (July 27, 1881), he writes: "I am absolutely not the kind of person who lives into his daily life like an animal in human form; I follow a particular goal, an ideal goal: knowledge (or intuitive cognition, *Erkenntnis*) of the truth." No wonder, as we learn further, he is already trying to bring his "Philosophy of Freedom" onto paper: "To strive for the Absolute, this human yearning is for truth."

Most importantly, during this whole period, he was continuously drawing closer to Goethe and to his mentor Karl Julius Schröer. It was a most fruitful relationship, but a paradoxical one. Steiner learned much from his mentor and enjoyed a unique closeness with him, but their paths would diverge. Steiner knew that his task was fundamentally different from Schröer's. In fact, in a way, it was the very difference in their orientations, coexisting as they did within a framework of mutual trust and respect, that was Schröer's greatest intellectual gift to Steiner. As he puts it in his *Autobiography*:

> Everything from Schröer was spiritually congenial to me. Nevertheless even in relation to him, I had to independently establish the more intimate aspects of what I worked for spiritually. Schröer was an idealist; for him, the driving force in everything created, whether by nature or humanity, was the world of ideas itself. For me, on the other hand, ideas were shadows cast by a living spiritual world. Yet I found it difficult to say, even for myself, what the difference was between Schröer's way of thinking and my own. He spoke of ideas as the forces driving history. He felt that ideas have life. For me the life of spirit was behind ideas.

Steiner called his view "objective idealism," and it was important to him to be able to harmonize it with "scientific" knowledge of the sensory world. Thus gradually, even before working closely with Goethe's approach to science, Steiner was wrestling with the relationship between the spiritual and physical worlds. Committed to the rigor of modern scientific thinking and recognizing its epochal nature in the evolution of human consciousness, he also recognized the profound, potentially lethal dangers of its materialistic view of human beings and the world, which dismissed as non-existent the non-material realities that he knew to be primary. As for what Goethe might offer to resolve his quandaries, Schröer could not help. He was not a scientist; and, though he knew Goethe's poetry, dramas, and fictions intimately, and perhaps better than anyone, Goethe's scientific writings remained a cryptic and closed book to him. Steiner would have to make his own way there.

But destiny was already preparing for that. In his study of optics and light, he found that, following his own spiritual insights and conducting experiments based on them, without knowing it he was drawing close to Goethe's theory of color: that light is a bridge between sensory and suprasensory realities. This, in turn, led him to consider other sciences, such as anatomy and physiology, from the same approach.

Thus, as he puts it, he was led in his own way to Goethe's theory of metamorphosis. He was beginning to see how the physical world related to the spiritual world. However, there was no one—not even Schröer—with whom he could talk about his discoveries. Whenever he did so, what he was saying was taken to be just theory. He found solace, however, in re-reading the famous exchange between Goethe and Schiller, in which Goethe "sketched" the archetypal plant for Schiller; and Schiller responded by calling it "not an experience but just an idea," a mere "theory;" to which Goethe replied, "If it's an idea, I see it with my eyes." With this inspiration, Steiner was converted, and turned to a detailed study of Goethe's scientific writings.

Soon thereafter, destiny strangely confirming his decision, Rudolf Steiner was invited on Schröer's recommendation to edit Goethe's scientific writings for the Kürschner edition of Goethe's collected works. It was 1882. Rudolf Steiner was twenty-one years old. As he wrote: "For me this task meant that I had to come to terms with both natural science and Goethe's worldview. Since it would be presented to the public, I also had to reach a certain conclusion about what I had attained at that point about my own worldview."

Goethe's great contribution was that, in contrast to conventional science's mechanist-materialist bias toward—indeed, nearly exclusive focus upon—what was lifeless, or dead, Goethe's orientation was toward Life. He sought what was living and he understood that life, which was continuous and whole, permeated and included all in its embrace. His central discovery therefore, we might say, was how to think about and affirm the primacy of the organic. As Steiner put it: "What Galileo did for inorganic nature, Goethe attempted to do for organic nature." This required a completely different approach. Rather than linking concepts together in a logically plausible, mathematically expressible, causal sequence, thinking about living nature required an organic, holistic, intuitive-participatory approach in which what the senses revealed as a sequence of parts is instead allowed to unfold in a single, continuous, unified process of metamorphosis. In Steiner's words, "When cognizing the organic, one concept must be allowed to grow out of the other so that, in the progressing, living transformation of concepts, images arise that display the being formed in nature." It was one thing, however, to identify Goethe's method, but it was quite another to account for it epistemologically. He had set himself both tasks. Both would be long and arduous in their completion, but the rewards and the gifts would be great, and would prepare him in ways he could not imagine for the larger, world-spiritual tasks that lay ahead.

During the first year (1882-1883), he managed to complete the introductions to the first volume, which contained Goethe's writings on the related realities of metamorphosis and morphology. To undertake such a project required both a thorough immersion into Goethe's work and a first foray into the alchemical—Paracelsian and Rosicrucian—sources that provided Goethe with the unspoken orientation within which his own innate powers of observation, perception, intuition, and thinking would operate. We may imagine then that a deepening and meditative familiarity with these sources allowed Steiner, following Goethe's example, to begin his own philosophical and epistemological evolutionary transformation of the esoteric traditions of hermetic sacred science. Not that Steiner could ever speak openly about such matters. To do so would have inevitably shipwrecked any chance that either the Goethean or his own worldview would be taken seriously.

Thus we find him beginning his Introductions by stating that the great discovery, which framed Goethe's study of nature, was "the discovery of the nature of the organism itself." For Goethe, organisms or "living beings" are the forms, or unities, through which life manifests; and life in a sense is synonymous with organism, so that, for Goethe, the idea of organism (or life) extends far beyond the forms of ordinary biological life—in some sense, everything is life, everything lives, and the concept of organism extends to include the universe itself: the organism of organisms. Not surprisingly, when it comes to explaining this, we find Steiner choosing his words very carefully with regard to Goethe's sources of inspiration, which, since known, must be admitted. He writes of the idea of the universe conceived of as a living being:

> This concept originates, of course, in Goethe's alchemical studies ... and in his reading of Paracelsus after returning from Leipzig

> [1768-1769], when he attempted through some kind of experiment, to reveal the principle that permeates the whole universe and to bring it to manifestation through some substance. But this way of looking at the world, bordering on the mystical, constitutes only a passing episode in Goethe's development and soon gives way to a healthier, more objective way of thinking...

Certainly Goethe's practical, laboratory experiences with alchemy were relatively short-lived; but Steiner makes clear, as Goethe's own work does, that, as Goethe matured and made his own path, nature herself became his laboratory, allowing him to transform alchemical language into the language of phenomenological observation.

Following a short introductory statement, the first two chapters of Steiner's contribution to the first volume deal largely biographically with Goethe's accomplishments in understanding plant and animal metamorphosis. The third chapter then considers the significance of Goethe's understanding of morphology. This was a field that Goethe virtually invented. Steiner calls it "a scientific accomplishment of the highest order," because for the first time it lays down the scientific foundations for studying organic nature. Inorganic nature we more or less understand because what is given to the senses (directly or through instrumentation) is immediately transformable into concepts. The phenomena and the ensuing concepts are more or less interchangeable: there is nothing in the one that is not in the other. In other words, we do not have to go beyond the sensory world to understand it. Goethe's breakthrough was to realize that, to understand the organic world, we have to go beyond what the senses give us: to perceive is not sufficient, we must somehow grasp the unifying principle. One cannot say, for example, that a plant's roots "determine" its leaves or blossoms. There is a relationship—accessible through a higher unity—but it is not causal in the same way that phenomena (for instance, classically, billiard balls) appear causally related in the inorganic world. To understand the inorganic world depends upon cognizing the higher unity, which Kant deemed to be impossible. But Goethe, knowing Kant to be wrong, discovered Spinoza, who spoke of *scientia intuitiva* or "knowledge in beholding." He called it "judgment through intuitive perception" and worked assiduously to develop within himself the capacity for such heightened seeing. This meant learning to see the becoming of an organism in its wholeness.

Goethe himself claimed never to have thought about thinking. In his essay "The Influence of the New Philosophy," he wrote:

> As vegetation demonstrated its method to me step by step, I could not possibly go astray, and by letting vegetation tell its own story, I necessarily became acquainted with its ways and means of developing to completion the most obscure phenomena.
>
> In my study of physics I gained the conviction that one's highest duty in observing phenomena is to trace accurately every condition under which a phenomenon makes its appearance.
>
> Kant's *Critique of Pure Reason* had long since appeared, but it lay completely beyond my orbit. Nevertheless, I was present at many a discussion of it, and with some attentiveness I could notice the old question continually reappearing; namely, how much do we, and how much does the outside world, contribute to our intellectual existence? I had never separated the two, and when I did philosophize about subjects in my own way, I did so with unconscious naïveté, in the belief that I actually saw my views before my very eyes....

It was therefore up to Steiner to provide the epistemological (philosophical) foundation.

The first volume of the Kürschner edition of Goethe's scientific writings, containing the morphological works and Steiner's introductions to them, appeared in 1884. Steiner was now twenty-three. He had just found a position as live-in tutor to the Specht children, which provided him not only with profound experiences in the art of education and child development (which would later bear rich fruit in Waldorf education), but also with a friendly, congenial home life within a family. Here, in tandem with preparing the second volume of Goethe's scientific writings, he wrote his own first book, *Goethe's Theory of Knowledge*, which would be published October 1886 by W. Speman in Berlin and Stuttgart, a year and a half after he began it.

Given how much else Steiner was doing, this was an extraordinary, even virtuoso performance, profound and far-reaching in its consequences. After all, it laid the ground for all of his subsequent work. Reading it therefore demands from its readers a like kind of virtuosity. It is not an easy book. Like *The Philosophy of Freedom*, it is not so much an exposition of something worked out beforehand, as it is the living experience of a way of knowing being worked out before us. It requires that we think along with Steiner, in a kind of extended "thought-experiment," to see what happens. It must not therefore be read, for information of any kind, but slowly and thoughtfully (meditatively), always with an eye for what is unthought and always remembering that, in a way, it is perhaps not so much about Goethe's path of knowing, as it is about Steiner's own embryonic path. Not that it is *not* about Goethe but, bearing in mind that Goethe "never thought about thinking," it rather develops and extends what is unthought (unarticulated) in Goethe: it is the philosophy or epistemology he never wrote. As Steiner puts it, what he was trying to do was to unfold "a development of what manifested in Goethe as a scientific sense—an interpretation of his way of observing the world." Thus, the book concerns the relationship between observer and the world; between the world of consciousness and ideas and the real, phenomenal world as it appears to our senses.

Steiner begins by distinguishing "thinking" and "experience." Thinking arises in response to experience, which to begin with he defines as what is given through the senses. Experience in this form is the unadulterated sensory comprehension of reality, and we respond to it with various kinds of mental classification. We impose names, concepts, and so forth upon our initially "pure" experience. We still call it experience—the experience of the color red, for instance—but actually the experience of the world as classified is already a mixture of pure experience and thinking. Pure experience in itself only exists if we exclude ourselves. Nevertheless, what arises is not subject to our control and bears some relationship to the phenomena we call colors, tones, trees, and so on.

Turning to the inner world, he finds it manifests a similar process. Inwardly, again, something arises as an experience, and we sense it. Therefore we may enlarge our notion of experience and say that all experience is sensed experience: it is what "appears" either to the outer or inner senses. In fact, if we pay attention to inner experience, we will observe that thought—thinking—too first appears to inner sense as experience, but with a crucial difference. As Steiner puts it, "In thinking, what we have to look for with the rest of experience has itself become direct experience." That is, thinking is immediate, transparent experience. Examining it, that is, separating it from ourselves, we are forced to recognize, however, that it likewise arises from an unknown source, just as outer sensory experience does. True thinking is thus essentially contemplation: it is directed to what exists before it, to something given; a world process. That is to say: "Before we can gain a deeper understanding of the world through thinking, thought must itself become experience." We must learn to discern the pure experience in thought, for only by doing so can we find the coherent bridge between thinking and the sensory world.

Experience, however, before it encounters thinking, is chaotic: a mere buzzing confused flow; a juxtaposition or sequence of unrelated particulars. That is to say: it is initially apparently formless, and only through thinking does experience acquire form, harmony, lawfulness or internal cohesion. And, furthermore, only though thinking does experience—what is given to us from the world—become ours. But this is not to say that the qualities revealed through thinking are "subjective"—either physiologically or in any other way. What is given is "objective"—real. The fact that some people believe it to be subjective arises only through erroneous thinking.

Having established the basis of "experience," Steiner then goes deeper in his phenomenological exploration to consider the notion that thinking itself is also experience, but of a higher order. The difference is that in thinking—as thinking becomes experience, or is transparently sensed—the experience of thinking is, in fact, always whole, lawful, and harmonious. Furthermore, it does not enter from "outside" in any spatial sense, but arises only through our participation in its becoming. The fact is that experience is essentially misunderstood. It is mistakenly separated from thinking, as thinking is from "reality"; whereas, in fact, thinking, as an experience of the real, is the highest, most direct experience we can have. Thinking and experience in this sense are one, and therefore a Goethean view emphasizes the need to remain true to experience—to the continuum or continuity. Goethe's is a true empiricism of consciousness.

Here one must be clear: what Steiner means by thinking is not just having thoughts. Thinking is the living, holistic, independent, and universal reality. It is the ground of experience, of which our thoughts are only the accompanying trace: the residues of our having participated in it. All of this is to say that the so-called sensory world and the so-called world of thinking or consciousness are, as it were, two sides of a single reality. In other words, thinking is not subjective; it is what we "produce" by our own effort as an act of participation in the world process. It consciously reunites what is split in two by our sensory-physiological-neurological organization.

To articulate this process, Steiner first has recourse to the distinction, made popular by Kant, between two levels of thinking: intellect (*Verstand*) and reason (*Vernünft*). The intellect divides. Its world is the world of the many or of multiplicity. Continuously separating, it creates concepts, dualities: cause and effect, mechanism and organism, freedom and necessity, and so on. Reason, on the other hand, apprehends unities, uniting separative concepts through unitive ideas. Overcoming the intellect's world of separation and disconnected, fragmented multiplicity, reason restores harmony and wholeness. It returns cognition to reality, which is self-evidently whole. Reason (*Vernünft*) in this sense is thus closer to the wisdom of the heart than to the cerebration of the head. Yet Kant condemned the unity achieved by reason as mere subjectivity. He failed to understand—or could not philosophically account for—the truths of intuition. For Kant, the unity that *Vernünft* achieved was illusory; it was simply the result of a subjective desire for order. Ideas, for Kant, had significance only for our human systems of knowledge; they had nothing to do with the world. But for Steiner (and Goethe) the cognitive function of reason is co-creatively and intuitively to reveal real unities.

The key lies in the act of cognition. We seem to be faced with two separate spheres: experience and thinking. On the one hand, reality, apart from thinking, appears in the form of experience. On the other hand, the nature of ordinary human knowing is outwardly directed:

what it works with is given through experience. But does experience contain the essential nature of a thing? Most often, in the case of sensory experience, the essential nature of a thing is only revealed through subsequent mental activity. But in the case of thinking, that is, cognition, the essential nature seems to be given directly. The critical task, then, is to overcome this duality and find one's way to a non-dualistic epistemology.

Steiner's (and Goethe's) approach to the riddle of cognition—or knowing—which, since Descartes at least, has always been split by the apparent abyss between the world and human thought, depends upon the realization that "our mind should not be regarded as a receptacle for the ideas containing the thoughts within itself, but as an organ that perceives these thoughts"—that is, as an organ that perceives thinking. In other words: "The mind is no less an organ of apprehension than are the eyes and the ears. Thought is related to our mind as light is related to the eye and sound to the ear." Cognition is analogous to perception. Like light, the reality that thinking cognizes is self-determined and whole. Therefore it is far from subjective or limited to individual minds. Each mind cognizes the same reality: as Steiner puts it, "there is only a single thought-content of the world." The world and thinking are non-dual.

"Thought," in other words, "is the essential nature of the world." "Everything is resolved in thought and eventually finds its place there." The fundamental reality of the world is thinking or consciousness, which comes to self-consciousness or is realized through us, that is, through thinking. "To presume a fundamental source of being outside the idea is absurd," Steiner concludes at the close of the first part of his study and continues:

> The whole source of being has poured itself out into the world; it has merged with it. It reveals itself in its most perfect form as thought, just as it is in itself. Consequently, if thinking makes a connection or a judgment, it is the essence of the ground of the world itself, poured into thought, that unites with it...Through thinking, we lift ourselves from perceiving reality as a product to perceiving reality as something that produces.

With this, Steiner turns to the applications of the epistemology he has worked out: that is, how, actually, Goethe did science. He begins with inorganic nature (ordinary physics and chemistry), where everything in the apparent relationships between phenomena or events is already given: one fact or event is always the result of other similar facts or events. Here, using trial and error, thought arranges events and conditions so as to achieve transparent clarity in results. Clarity of thought achieves experimental clarity. As we stand transparently within thought, a similar transparency appears in the phenomena. The sensory world appears "as a web of simple facts that the mind can penetrate and simplify." But for Goethe (and Steiner) this is only the beginning. For, obviously, not all phenomena or relationships are equal; one has much greater universality than others. It is, in effect, a constant and constitutes "a higher experience within experience." With regard to the inorganic realm, Steiner calls it the "elemental phenomenon," the basic fact: that is, the experiment. The experiment is simultaneously "objective"—"we arrange certain conditions whose nature and what follows we observe"—and subjective, in that we thought it out. In other words, using Goethe's words, in inorganic science, "experiment is the mediator between subject and object."

Organic or living nature is something else entirely. The understanding of life has eluded modern science from its beginnings and, truth be told, as far as conventional biology goes, it still does. Scientists still do not know what life is, any more than they know what consciousness is. Goethe, however, was committed to understanding both the unitary living, evolving, ever-transforming Proteus that he called Life, and consciousness, which is but a metamorphosis of it. He understood that—even though they were the only ones touted as properly scientific—the methods developed for the inorganic world treated as a "finished" realm of "dead" conceptual objects could not be applied to the organic realm, which was not finished, and certainly not dead, but in a process of perpetual becoming. However, he was unwilling on this account to assume that it could not be understood. Kant had limited the study of organisms to whatever purposes or intents one could abstract from them: in other words, to conceptual—and inevitably partial and fragmented—descriptions of behavior. Goethe found this insufferably superficial. He was interested in the essential inner nature of a thing; not how it is used, but how it evolved: what perfection it seeks. Recognizing intuitively both that method was not extraneous to its field of application and, conversely, that knowledge was a function of method, Goethe knew intuitively that every field of inquiry required a different and appropriate method of investigation. Life, which is fluid, requires a fluidity of approach. Some kind of evolutionary participation must take the place of logical, concept-driven proof.

As an example, Steiner points to Goethe's use of the "type." The type is what appears in the particular with the form of the general. Not perfectly developed in any single organism, the type is present (immanent) in all related organisms. It is not fixed, but mobile. While it is, on the one hand, the *idea* of an organism—what makes it what it is, the general or universal in the particular—it is, on the other hand, not, at least in the first place, any kind of Platonic Form or Archetype. Rather, it is what we can grasp from a laborious and attentive observation of phenomenal particulars. As Steiner puts it: "The type is the inner aspect of what we experience as the outer forms of living creature."

In the organic world, then, type plays the same role as law (the elemental phenomenon) does in the inorganic world.

To grasp or "see" a type requires not simply judgment and reflection, but intuitive vision (judgment and perception). That Goethe sought to reach scientific truths by means of intuition has been held against him. Nevertheless, as Steiner shows, for the organic world, intuition is the correct, indeed the only possible, method. The limits of logic are neither world limits (the world is not reducible to what is logically provable), nor are the limits of logic the limits of what we can know. Logical proof or dialectical thinking is, in fact, often but a substitute for the true insight of intuition. Through it, we are enabled to think within the thinking that thinks in and through nature. Kant is overcome.

Having established a Goethean approach to the sciences, Steiner turns to the humanities: the spiritual or cultural sciences. The key here is the self-determining, individual nature of human existence: in a word, *human freedom*, the "I." Through freedom, the world becomes spiritualized. Such freedom has been, in fact, the golden thread running through the entire work, whose aim, as Steiner confesses at the end, has been to strip away the passivity often associated with cognition and to affirm in its place the creativity of the human spirit. Human knowing is no mirrored representation. On the contrary, free human cognitive creativity leads us much "more deeply into the true fabric of the world than does any analysis and observation of the external world as mere experience." Read in this light, *Goethe's Theory of Knowledge*, in addition to being a significant epistemological achievement, is an inspiring affirmation of human freedom.

---

*To be quite clear: *Outlines of an Epistemological Theory of the Goethean Worldview with a Special Consideration of Schiller*, here published as *Goethe's Theory of Knowledge* was Rudolf Steiner's first independent publication in book form. It was at the same time published as a supplement to Kürschner's collection of Goethe's scientific works in *German National-Literature*. Chronologically, its publication comes between the first (1884) and the second (1887) volumes of the five volumes of *Goethe's Scientific Writings*. The book of ninety-two pages first appeared in October 1886 from the publisher W. Speman, Berlin and Stuttgart (2,000 copies were printed). It received some reviews. The second edition (4,000 copies), with a new Foreword, Annotations, and a few textual changes, appeared in December 1923 (with the publication date of 1924) from Der Kommenden Tag Press in Stuttgart. This formed the basis of the final edition (4,000 copies), overseen and corrected by Rudolf Steiner, published in 1924 by the Philosophisch-Anthroposophisch Verlag am Goetheanum in Dornach.

GOETHE'S THEORY
OF KNOWLEDGE

Rudolf Steiner

## *Preface to the Edition of 1924*

THIS STUDY OF the theory of knowledge implied in Goethe's world-view was written between 1880 and 1890. At the time, my mind was engaged in two directions; on the one hand, I tried to formulate the view of life and the world that motivated Goethe's work. I saw the fully and purely human aspect of everything Goethe gave to the world through his creative work, through reflection, and through his life. It seemed to me that his work represented inner assurance, harmonious wholeness, and a sense of reality in relation to the world more than anything else in the modern age did. With this in mind, I could see clearly that Goethe's method of cognition arises from the very nature of the human being and the world.

My thoughts also focused on the prevailing philosophical concepts regarding the essential nature of knowing. Such views held that knowledge showed every sign of confinement to the human being. The brilliant philosopher Otto Liebmann[†] had asserted that human consciousness cannot go beyond itself and therefore must remain within itself. Human consciousness can know nothing of true reality beyond the world that consciousness forms within itself. In brilliant writings Otto Liebmann elaborated this thinking with respect to the many facets of human experience. Johannes Volkelt[†] had written two thoughtful books: *Kant's Theory of Knowledge* and *Experience and Thinking*. He saw human perception of the world as merely a combination of mental pictures based on the relationship between the human being and an unknown world. He acknowledged, however, that a necessity arises in the area of mental pictures in our inner experience of thinking. In the process of thinking, we have a sense of, as it were, forcing our way through the world of mental pictures into the world of reality. However, what do we gain from this? We could feel justified in forming judgments about the real world, but through such judgments, we do not go beyond ourselves and do not actually perceive the nature of the world.

Eduard von Hartmann†—whose philosophy had been of great service to me despite the fact that I could not agree with its fundamental presuppositions or conclusions—maintained exactly the same point of view as Volkelt regarding the theory of knowledge. Everyone acknowledged that human knowledge reaches certain barriers that prevent entry into the realm of true reality.

In opposition to all this, I asserted that, if we deepen our thinking sufficiently, we can live in a spiritual reality that we experience inwardly and recognize in life. I believed that I possessed this spiritual knowledge with the same clarity of consciousness that characterizes mathematical knowledge. In the presence of such knowledge, it is impossible to maintain the opinion that the limitations of cognition exist as asserted in the philosophical reasoning mentioned here.

In relation to all this, I tended somewhat toward the theory of evolution then in full flower. For Haeckel, this theory had developed in such a way that it completely dismissed self existent being and spiritual activity. The later and more perfect being was thought to arise in time from the earlier and undeveloped. This was evident to me in the external reality of the senses, but I was too well aware of the self existing spiritual—based on its own foundation and independent of the senses—to assign credence only to what appears to the outer world of the senses. Nonetheless, a bridge had to be established between this world and the spiritual world.

In the course of time, as perceived by the senses, the spiritual in the human being seems to have evolved from what was previously non-spiritual. However, the sensory world, when correctly perceived, manifests everywhere as a revelation of the spiritual. In the light of this true knowledge of the sensory world, I saw clearly that "boundaries of knowledge," as then defined, could exist only for those who cannot know what lies beyond the physical world, just as someone might insist that a page of printed words is impossible to decipher merely because one has not taken the time to learn the forms of the letters.

Consequently, my attention was directed toward a path from sensory observation to the spiritual, which was firmly established in my inner experience of cognition. Behind sensory appearance I did not seek non-spiritual worlds of atoms; rather, I looked for the spirit that seems to reveal itself within the human being but actually belongs to the objects and processes of the sensory world itself. Because of our attitude in the act of knowing, it seems as though our thoughts about things exist in ourselves, whereas they really exist within the things themselves. Human beings feel a need to separate seemingly experienced thoughts from the things; in a true experience of knowing, we return thoughts to the things.

World evolution, therefore, should be understood in such a way that the previously nonspiritual, out of which human spirituality later develops, includes a spiritual element beside and outside of itself. The subsequent materiality imbued with spirit, in which the human being appears, then arises through one's spiritual ancestor having united with incomplete, nonspiritual forms and, by transforming them, appearing in a sensorially perceptible form. This train of ideas led me beyond the epistemologists of that time, whose acumen and scientific responsibility I fully recognized. It led me to Goethe.

Today I must think back to my inner struggles at that time. I did not make it easy for myself to go beyond the course of ideas in the prevailing philosophies, but my guiding star was always my inner recognition that human beings can view themselves as spirits, inwardly independent of the body and existing in a purely spiritual world.

Prior to my work with Goethe's scientific writings, and before this theory of knowing, I wrote a little essay on atomism, which was never published.[†] It followed the direction indicated here. I remember the joy with which I received words of agreement from Theodor Vischer, to whom I had sent the essay. Now, however, through my studies of Goethe it became clear how my thoughts were leading to a perception of the nature of knowledge that pervaded his work and attitude toward the world. I found that my own point of view gave me the epistemology found in Goethe's worldview.

During the 1880s, Karl Julius Schröer,[†] my teacher and fatherly friend to whom I am greatly indebted, recommended that I write the introductions to Goethe's scientific writings for Kürschner's *National-Literatur* and to take care of their publication. In this work, I followed

Goethe's life in all the areas of knowledge in which he was active. It became increasingly clear to me that, in every respect, my own views placed me within the epistemology in Goethe's worldview. Thus, I wrote this theory of knowledge during the course of completing that work.

In placing it before me again today, as a theory of knowledge it seems to form the basis and justification for everything I have said and published since then. It discusses a way of knowing that opens a path from the sensory world to a spiritual one.

It may seem unusual that this work from my youth, written almost forty years ago, appears again today, unchanged except for some added annotations. In its manner of presentation, it bears the marks of a kind of thinking prevalent in the philosophy of that time; if I were writing it today, I would say some things differently, though I could not describe knowing in any other way. But what I would write today could not as faithfully carry within it the seeds of the spiritual worldview I developed later. One can write in such a seminal way only at the beginning of one's path of knowledge. Consequently, this early work is allowed to reappear with its form unchanged. What existed as theories of knowledge when it was written have been continued in later theories. What I had to say about it was stated in my book *The Riddles of Philosophy*,† which will be issued simultaneously in a new edition by the same publishers. What I outlined years ago as the epistemology implicit in Goethe's worldview seems just as necessary to say now as it was forty years ago.

Rudolf Steiner
The Goetheanum
Dornach, November 1923

## *Foreword to the First Edition (1886)*

When Professor Kürschner honored me by entrusting me with the task of editing Goethe's scientific writings for the *Deutsche National-Literatur*, I was fully aware of the difficulties confronting me in such an undertaking. I would need to oppose a perspective that had become established almost universally.

The belief that Goethe's poetic writings are the basis of our whole culture is gaining ground everywhere, whereas even those who give the greatest recognition to his scientific writings see them as no more than premonitions of facts confirmed more fully with scientific progress. Because of his innate insight (as it is held in limited regard), he was able to anticipate natural laws that were rediscovered later through independent and strictly scientific methods. While every well-informed person greatly admires Goethe's other works, his scientific view is not as well regarded. It is certainly not acknowledged that, by becoming familiar with the scientific works of that poet, we can gain something that science would not otherwise provide.

When my beloved teacher Karl Julius Schröer introduced me to Goethe's worldview, my thinking had already been inclined in such a way that I could direct my attention to the most important point: the way in which Goethe enmeshed such a singular discovery into his whole view of nature, and the way he used his discovery to understand the interrelationships of the beings of nature, or (to use the striking expression of Goethe himself in his paper "Anschauende Urteilskraft")*† in order to participate spiritually in natural manifestations. I soon recognized that the achievements that contemporary science attributes to Goethe were not essential, whereas his truly significant achievements were overlooked. Those singular discoveries truly could have been made without Goethe's research, but science would lack his lofty view of nature so long as this view is not derived from Goethe himself.

This was how I determined the direction of my introductions for the edition.* They must show that each of Goethe's expressed opinions should be derived from the totality of his genius.

The principles necessary to accomplish this make up the substance of this brief treatise, which tries to show that our presentation of Goethe's scientific views can be established as self-evident.

With this, I have said all that seemed necessary to preface the following discussion, except to discharge a pleasing duty: the expression of my most heartfelt thanks to Professor Kürschner, who has given his friendly help in writing this little book with the same good will that he has always shown toward my scientific endeavors.

Rudolf Steiner
The end of April, 1886

# A : Preliminary Questions

## 1. The Point of Departure

When we trace any one of the main streams of spiritual life today back to its source, we always arrive at a great spirit of our "classical age." Goethe, Schiller, Herder, or Lessing gave an impulse, and from that impulse arose an intellectual movement that continues today. Many who consider themselves entirely original achieve no more than an expression of what was suggested long ago by Goethe or Schiller—to the degree that all of German culture is founded upon classical authors from that era. We have aligned ourselves so closely with what the world has created through those classical authors that anyone who veers from the path shown by them can scarcely expect to be understood. They have determined our way of viewing life and the world to such a degree that only those who seek points of reference to this foundation can arouse our sympathetic interest.

We have to acknowledge that only one branch of our intellectual life has not yet found such a point of contact—the branch of knowledge that goes beyond a mere collection of observations, beyond the cognizance of single experiences, providing a satisfyingly complete view of the world and of life. It is generally called *philosophy*, an activity which in our "classical period" actually seems nonexistent. These days, philosophy seeks its salvation in arbitrary seclusion and aristocratic isolation from all the rest of our intellectual life. This assertion does not contradict the fact that many philosophers and scientists have devoted themselves to Goethe and Schiller, despite the fact that such modern thinkers have not developed their scientific perspectives from the foundation of the scientific works of those spiritual heroes. Rather, they arrived at their scientific standpoints independently of the worldviews of Goethe and Schiller, and only later connected them. Moreover, they did this not to find guidance in the scientific opinions of the great thinkers, but merely to test those opinions and discover whether they would hold up in the face of their own course of reasoning. We will address this point later on more thoroughly. First, however, we would like to point out how this attitude toward the highest stage of development in contemporary culture affects the field of philosophy.

Much of today's educated reading public will not read any scientific literature that makes philosophical claims. Seldom has philosophy enjoyed such little favor as it does today. Except for the writings of Schopenhauer and Eduard von Hartmann—which, because they deal with the broadest questions of life and the world, have gained a wide circulation—it is safe to say that philosophical works are read today only by professional philosophers. Aside from them, no one bothers with such writings. Educated nonspecialists have the vague feeling that such writings contain nothing of intellectual worth and that the matters discussed in them are of no concern and are unrelated to real spiritual needs. This lack of interest in philosophy must be a result of the circumstance I mentioned; in face of such indifference, there is an ever-increasing need for a satisfying view of the world and life. Religious dogmas, which provided an adequate long-standing substitute, are increasingly losing their power to convince. Pressure is growing steadily to employ thinking to attain what humanity previously attained through faith in revelation: satisfaction of the spirit. Thus, the interest of cultured people would not be missing if this particular branch of knowledge kept pace with the evolution of culture as a whole, and if its representatives would take a position on the great questions that move humanity.

Here, we must always bear in mind that it can never be a matter of arbitrarily creating a spiritual need, but only of seeking out and satisfying the need that exists. The task of science is not to raise questions; rather, it is to give careful attention and answers to the questions presented by human nature and by the current stage of evolution. The tasks that modern philosophers take up do not flow out of the present stage of culture, and thus they are questions to which no one is seeking answers. Science passes over the questions that our culture must ask and to which our great thinkers have led the way. Thus, we have a science that no one seeks and a scientific need that no one satisfies.

Our central branch of knowledge ought to solve the real mysteries of the world for us, and it must not be an exception in relation to all other branches of the intellectual life. It must look for its sources where the other branches of knowledge have found them. Philosophy must not only recognize the great classical thinkers, but also seek in them the foundation for its own evolution. It must breathe the same air as does the rest of our culture. This necessity is inherent in the very nature of things, notwithstanding the fact that modern researchers have tried to interpret our classical writers as we have explained. However, such interpretations reveal no more than a vague sense that it is inappropriate simply to ignore the convictions of those thinkers and proceed with the order of the day. Nonetheless, these interpretations also show that such opinions really have not been developed. This modern approach to Lessing, Herder, Goethe, and Schiller demonstrates this fact. Despite the excellence of many such endeavors, it must be understood that these writings on the scientific works of Schiller and Goethe were not developed organically from their views but have merely a retrospective relationship to them. Nothing substantiates this more strongly than the fact that diverse representatives of science have seen premonitions of their own points of view in the genius of Goethe. Representatives of worldviews that share nothing in common refer to Goethe with seemingly equal justification, especially when they feel a need to see their various views recognized as the height of human endeavor. One can scarcely imagine a sharper contrast than that between the teachings of Hegel and Schopenhauer. The latter calls Hegel a charlatan[†] and his philosophy a shallow concoction of words, mere nonsense, and barbaric combinations of words. The two men actually share nothing except their unlimited admiration for Goethe,[†] as well as their belief that Goethe professed adherence to their respective worldviews.

The case is no different for more recent scientific directions. Haeckel, who sympathetically elaborated Darwinism with an ironclad logic, and whom we must consider by far the most significant follower of the English investigator, sees the anticipation of his own view in that of Goethe.† Another contemporary scientific investigator, K.F.W. Jessen,[1] writes of Darwin's theory: "The stir created among many research specialists and nonspecialists by this theory—frequently presented and as often disproved previously by thorough investigation,[2] but now supported by many pretentious arguments†—shows, unfortunately, how little the results of scientific research are generally known and understood." Concerning Goethe, the same investigator says that he rose "to comprehensive research in both inanimate and animate nature" in that he found the fundamental law of all plant formation through a "thoughtful, deeply penetrating observation of nature."[3] Each of these two investigators is able to cite a wearisome number of proofs to show the harmony between his own scientific direction and the "thoughtful observations of Goethe," but, if each of these standpoints could justly refer to Goethe's thought, this must cast a dubious light upon the consistency of each respective mode of thinking. The reason for this seeming inconsistency, however, lies in the very fact that neither of these viewpoints really grows out of Goethe's worldview; rather, each has its roots quite outside that view. This situation arises from the fact that people look for external agreement in details torn from Goethe's thought as a whole—in which case they lose their meaning—while they are at the same time unwilling to consider the whole of Goethe's thought as fit to serve as the basis for a scientific trend of thought. Scientific research has always ignored Goethe's views as points of departure, using them instead as material to make comparisons. Those who have busied themselves with such views have seldom been students who open themselves with unbiased minds to his ideas, but more often as critics who pass judgment on him.

There are even those who say that Goethe had far too little scientific sense, that he was an even worse philosopher for being such an excellent poet, and that, because of this, it would be impossible to find in his work any foundation for a scientific perspective. This is a complete misconception of Goethe's nature. To be sure, Goethe was no philosopher in the ordinary sense of the term, but we should remember that the wonderful harmony of his personality led Schiller to declare, "The poet is the only true human being."† Goethe personified what Schiller meant by a "true human being." No element of the highest expression of the universal human was lacking in his personality; further, all of these elements came together in him to form a totality that acted as such in a powerful way. Thus, it happens that a profound philosophical sense forms the basis for his opinions about nature, even though this philosophical sense does not enter his consciousness in the form of specific scientific statements. Those who immerse themselves in this wholeness (provided they have philosophic capacities) will be able to reveal this philosophic sense and present it as Goethe's form of knowledge. But one must work with Goethe's works as a foundation and not approach him with a preconceived opinion. Goethe's intellectual powers could always deal appropriately with the strictest philosophy, even though he has not left such a philosophy behind as a complete system.

Goethe's worldview is the most multifaceted imaginable. It proceeds from a central point that lies in the unified nature of the poet, and it always brings out that aspect corresponding to the nature of the object under observation. A uniform activity of intellectual forces lies in the nature of Goethe; the given object determines the particular form of that activity. Goethe borrows his manner of observation from the external world and does not force his own upon it. The thinking of many people works only in one particular way; it serves only for a certain type of object—it is not unified, as was Goethe's, but only unitary. Let us endeavor to express this more exactly: there are people whose intellects are especially suited to think out merely mechanical interdependencies and effects. They conceive the entire universe as a mechanism. Others have the impulse to perceive everywhere the secret mystical element of the external world—they become adherents of mysticism. All sorts of errors arise when such thinking, though entirely valid for one class of objects, is declared universal. This explains the conflicts among various worldviews. If such a lopsided view confronts that of Goethe (which is unlimited because it takes its manner of observation not from the mind of the observer, but from the nature of the thing observed), then we can easily see how this lopsided view clings to the element of thought that harmonizes with its own. Goethe's worldview includes, in the sense just indicated, many directions of thought, though it can never be penetrated by means of a one-sided concept.

The philosophical sense, which is an essential element of Goethe's genius, is also significant for his poetry. Though it was alien to Goethe to present in clear conceptual form what was mediated to him by this sense, as Schiller did, it was nonetheless an active factor in his artistic, creative work, as it was for Schiller. The poetic productions of Goethe and Schiller are unthinkable apart from their worldviews, which stood in the background. With Schiller, this is more a matter of concretely formulated basic principles, whereas for Goethe it was inherent in the way that he observed things. However, the fact that our nation's greatest poets at the peak of their creative work needed a philosophical element proves more than anything that such an element is a necessary constituent in the history of human development. It is precisely the support of Goethe and Schiller that will enable us to tear our central science (that is, philosophy) away from its academic isolation and incorporate it into the rest of our cultural evolution. The scientific convictions of our classical authors are bound by a thousand ties to their other endeavors; such was the demand of the cultural epoch they created.

# 2. Goethe's Science According to Schiller's Method

IN THE PRECEDING PAGES, we determined the direction to be taken in the following inquiries. These inquiries are to constitute a development of what manifested in Goethe as a scientific sense—an interpretation of his way of observing the world. One might argue that this is not the way to present a viewpoint scientifically; that authority must never, under any circumstances replace principles as the basis for scientific opinion. Let us immediately discuss this argument. We do not accept an opinion based upon Goethe's worldview simply because we can deduce it from that view, but because we believe Goethe's worldview can be supported by tenable basic principles and can be represented as a self-sustaining view. The fact that we begin with Goethe will not prevent us from being equally concerned with showing the basis for the opinions we maintain as are the exponents of any science claiming to be free of preconceptions. We represent Goethe's worldview, but we shall base it according to the requirements of science.

The road that such inquiries must take was indicated by Schiller. No one perceived the greatness of Goethe's genius so clearly. In his letters to Goethe, he held before him an image of Goethe's own being. In his letters on the aesthetic education of humankind,[†] he develops the ideal of the artist as he had recognized it in Goethe. Moreover, in his essay on naïve and sentimental poetry, Schiller describes the nature of true art as he had come to know it in Goethe's poetic works. This is our justification for designating that our discussion is built on the foundation of the Goethe-Schiller worldview. Its purpose is to consider the scientific thought of Goethe according to the method for which Schiller provided a model. Goethe's gaze is directed toward nature and life, and his manner of observation will be the subject of our discussion. Schiller's gaze is directed toward the mind of Goethe, and his method of observation in this process will be the ideal of our own method. In this way, we believe the scientific endeavors of Goethe and Schiller are made fruitful for the present age.

According to the customary scientific terminology, we must consider our work to be an epistemology. The questions discussed, however, will be very different from those usually posed by that branch of philosophy. We have seen why this is so; where similar inquiries appear today, they virtually always take Kant as their point of departure. It has been altogether overlooked in scientific circles that, aside from the epistemology established by the great thinker of Königsberg, there is at least the possibility of another trend of thought in this field; a trend which is no less capable than that of Kant in dealing profoundly with the facts.

At the beginning of the 1860s, Otto Liebmann stated that we must return to Kant[†] if we aspire to a worldview free of contradictions. This is why today we possess a Kantian literature almost beyond the possibility of survey. Nevertheless, this road will also fail to help elevate philosophical thinking, which will not play a role in our cultural life again until, instead of returning to Kant, it goes more deeply into the scientific views of Goethe and Schiller.

Now we will approach the basic questions of epistemology addressed in these preliminary remarks.

# 3. The Purpose of Our Science

GOETHE'S APT EXPRESSION is true of all knowledge: "Theory, in and of itself, is useless unless it leads us to believe in the interrelationship of phenomena."[†] Through science, we are always connecting discrete facts of experience. In inorganic nature, we perceive causes and effects as separate and look for their relationship in the appropriate particular scientific field. In the organic world we become aware of species and genera of organisms, and we endeavor to establish reciprocal relationships among them. A number of different cultural epochs of humanity appear before us in history, and we endeavor to learn the inner dependence of one evolutionary stage upon another. Thus, every branch of science has to work in some specific field of phenomena in the sense of the above quote from Goethe.

Each branch of science seeks to discover the interrelationships among the phenomena within its sphere. Nonetheless, there remains a great antithesis in our scientific endeavors: on one side is the world of ideas gained by the sciences; on the other are the objects upon which that world is based. There must be a branch of science that also clarifies the reciprocal relationships between these two realms. The rift between the ideal and the real world—the antithesis between idea and reality—constitutes the problem of this branch of science. We must also understand these contrasting elements in their reciprocal relationships.

The purpose of the discussion that follows is to seek these relationships. The facts of science, on the one hand, and nature and history, on the other, will be interrelated. What is the significance of the reflection of the external world in human consciousness? What is the relationship between our thinking about the objects of reality and these objects themselves?

# B : Experience

## 4. Establishing the Concept of Experience

Two areas exist separately from each other: our thinking and the objects that occupy our thoughts. These latter are designated (inasmuch as they are accessible to observation) as the content of experience. For the moment, we will not determine whether there are other objects of thought beyond our field of observation or of what type they may be. First, we must establish sharp boundaries between the two areas of experience and thinking. We must have before us a definite picture of experience before we investigate the nature of thinking.

What is experience? Everyone is conscious of the fact that our thoughts are kindled through a confrontation with reality. We encounter objects in space and time; we become aware of a manifold and multifaceted external world, and we live in a more or less richly developed inner world. All of this meets us in a form that is already complete; we play no role in its manifestation. As though it springs from an unknown beyond, reality initially presents itself to the understanding of our senses and mind. To begin with, we can do no more than allow our gaze to sweep over the multiplicity that meets us. Our initial activity is the sensory comprehension of reality. We must grasp firmly what is offered to the senses, because only this can be called pure experience.

Next, we immediately feel a need to penetrate, through mental classification, the endless multiplicity of forms, forces, colors, tones, and so on that appear to us. We try to explain the interrelationships of all the individual entities that we encounter. When an animal appears in a certain area, we inquire about the influence of that area on the life of the animal; when we see a stone begin to roll, we look for other related events. What happens in this way, however, is no longer pure experience; its source is twofold: experience and thinking.

Pure experience is the way reality appears to us when we encounter it to the complete exclusion of what we ourselves bring to it. The words Goethe used in his essay "Nature" may be applied to this form of reality: "We are surrounded and embraced by her. Uninvited and without warning, she takes us up into the round of her dance."† In terms of the objects of the external senses, this undeniable fact stares us in the face. A body initially appears as a complex of forms, colors, and sensations of heat and light that suddenly confront us as though they had sprung from an unknown elemental source.

Our assertion does not contradict the psychological conviction that the sensory world, as it exists before us, is essentially a product of the interaction between our own organism and an outer world of unknown molecules. Even if it were actually true that color, heat, etc., were no more than the way our organism is affected by the external world, the process that transforms the events of the external world into color, heat, and so on nevertheless exists entirely beyond our consciousness. Regardless of the role our organism plays in this, what appears to our thinking as the preexistent form of reality, not subject to our control—that is, experience—is not the molecular event; rather, it is those colors, tones, and such.

The matter is not as clear when it comes to our inner life. However, a more precise consideration will remove all doubt that our inner states appear on the horizon of our consciousness in the same form as do the phenomena and facts of the outer world. A feeling impresses itself upon me just as a sensation of light does. The fact that I connect it more closely with my own personality is not important from this perspective. We must go even further. Thought itself appears to us initially as experience. In the very act of examining our thought, we separate it from ourselves; we conceive its initial form as arising from an unknown source. This cannot be otherwise. Our thinking is contemplation, especially when we view its form as a separate activity in consciousness; its attention is directed outward to what exists before it. In doing this, its activity first comes to rest. It would look into emptiness, or nothingness, if something did not confront it.

Everything that becomes an object of knowledge must first accommodate itself to this form of confrontation. We are incapable of raising ourselves above this form. Before we can gain a deeper understanding of the world through thinking, thought must itself become experience. We must look for thought itself as a fact of experience. This is the only way that our worldview can avoid a loss of inner coherence. Such a loss would happen immediately if we tried to include an alien element. We face pure experience and look within it for the element that illuminates itself and the rest of reality.

# 5. Examining the Essence of Experience

LET US NOW CONSIDER pure experience. What is its essence in terms of consciousness that is not elaborated by our thinking? It is simply spatial juxtaposition and temporal sequence—a mere collection of unrelated particulars. None of the objects that arise and disappear have anything to do with any other. At this stage, none of the facts that enter our awareness and that we experience inwardly have any bearing upon one another. Here, the world is a multiplicity of equivalent phenomena. No thing or event plays a greater part in the world than any other object in this area of experience. Before one fact can have greater significance than any other, we must not merely observe phenomena but connect them to our thinking. A rudimentary organ of an animal, which may have no significance for its organic functioning, is no different than the most important organ of the animal's body. Such a distinction of greater or lesser importance becomes apparent only when we consider the relationships of the individual objects of observation; in other words, we must first *work with* our experience.

In terms of pure experience, a snail, which belongs to a lower level of organism, is equal to the most highly evolved animal. Degrees of perfection in organization are not apparent until we think conceptually and work on the multiplicity presented by experience. Similarly, from this perspective, Inuit culture and that of educated Europeans are no different. To pure experience, Caesar's significance in human history appears no greater than that of one of his soldiers. In the history of literature, Goethe stands no higher than Gottsched, so long as we are considering mere experiential reality.

At this level of consideration, the world appears to our minds as an absolutely flat surface; no part rises above any other; nothing has any distinction. Until the spark of thinking strikes this surface, we do not perceive elevations and depressions; nothing appears above or below the other. With thinking, everything assumes a certain form; lines run from one form to another, and the whole becomes a integral harmony.

The illustrations we have chosen seem to show clearly enough what we mean by differences in the significance of objects of perception (considered here as identical with the things of experience). This is what we mean by the knowledge that first arises when we consider the interrelationships of objects. This, we believe, prevents the argument that our experience reveals endless distinctions among its objects before thinking approaches them—that a red surface, for instance, is distinct from a green surface, even without the activity of thought. This is true, but anyone who would thus refute us has misunderstood our assertion entirely. This is precisely what we maintain: All that is presented to us by experience is an endless mass of discrete entities. These discrete entities must, of course, differ individually from one another; otherwise they would not appear to us as an endless, unrelated multiplicity. We do not mean that the phenomena are indistinguishable, but that, at the level of sensory perception, they are completely unrelated and lack meaning for our overall image of reality. It is only because we recognize this endless qualitative difference that we are driven to reach conclusions.

If we were met by a self-consistent unity composed of harmoniously ordered constituents, we could not speak of an indifferent relationship between the constituents of this unity. Anyone who would consider our comparison irrelevant for such a reason has failed to understand the real point of similarity. It would certainly be fallacious if we compared the perceptual world, with its endlessly varied forms, to the uniform monotony of a level plain. But our level plain was not intended to resemble the actual manifold world of phenomena, but rather the unified, total image that we have of that world before thinking has come in contact with it. After thinking has been activated, each discrete entity in the whole appears not as it was when mediated by mere experience, but now with its particular significance in relation to the whole of reality. At the same time, each phenomenon appears with characteristics that were absent in its initial experiential form.

According to our conviction, Johannes Volkelt has been remarkably successful in delineating within clear outlines what we are justified in calling pure experience. Five years ago (1881) he aptly described this in his book *Kant's Theory of Knowledge* (*Kants Erkenntnistheoris*).[4] In his latest publication, *Experience and Thinking* (*Erfahrung und Denken*),[5] he pursued the subject further. He did this, to be sure, in support of a viewpoint that is fundamentally different from ours and with a purpose essentially unlike that of this book. However, this does not prevent us from presenting his excellent description of pure experience.

Volkelt's description simply shows us the images that briefly pass before our awareness in a manner completely void of interrelationships. He says:[6]

> For example, my consciousness now has as its content the impression that I have worked diligently today. Immediately, the impression is linked to this: I can take a walk with a clear conscience; but suddenly the image appears of the door opening and the mail carrier entering. The mail carrier soon appears with outstretched hand, then with mouth opening, then doing the opposite; at the same time, there are all sorts of auditory impressions connected with the perceptual content of the opening mouth, as well as other impressions, such as rain beginning outside.[†] The image of the mail carrier vanishes from my consciousness, and other impressions enter one after another: grasping scissors, opening the letter, a feeling of reproach at the poor handwriting, visual images of the various written symbols, and, connected with these, manifold imaginative images and thoughts. Scarcely has this series ended, when the impression of having worked diligently reappears and—accompanied by discontent—awareness of the continuing rain. Then both of these vanish from my consciousness, and an impression emerges that a difficulty, believed to have been overcome in the day's work, has actually not been overcome; along with this comes impressions of free will, empirical necessity, responsibility, the value of virtue, absolute chance, incomprehensibility, and so on, and these combine with one another in varied and complicated ways—and so it continues.

With regard to a certain, limited period of time, this describes our actual experience: the form of reality in which thinking has no part at all.

One should not think that we would achieve a different result if, instead of an ordinary experience, we had described a scientific experiment or a particular natural phenomenon. In either case, what passes before our consciousness is made up of unrelated images. Only thinking leads to a connection of these.

We must also acknowledge a contribution from Dr. Richard Wahle in his pamphlet *Gehirn und Bewusstsein* [(Brain and consciousness) Vienna 1884].[†] He clearly indicates what is presented to us by experience stripped of any element of thought. What he describes as absolutely valid characteristics of outer and inner phenomena, however, is true only for the first stage of observation that we have described. According to Wahle, we know only spatial juxtaposition and temporal sequence. According to him, there can be no discussion of a relationship among phenomena that appear adjacent to or in sequence to one another. For example, somewhere there may be an inner relationship between a warm sunbeam and the warming of the stone, but we know nothing of a causal relationship; to us, it is clear only that the second fact comes after the first. Likewise, there may be, somewhere in a world inaccessible to us, an inner relationship between our physical brain-mechanism and our mental activity; but we know only that the two are parallel phenomena; we are not at all justified in assuming a causal relationship between the two.

Of course, when Wahle presents this statement as the ultimate truth of science, we must contest his assertion, although it is entirely true of the first form in which we become aware of reality.

Not only are outer phenomena and inner processes devoid of an interrelationship at this stage of knowledge, but our own personality is also a discrete unit in relation to the rest of the world. We perceive ourselves as one of the numberless percepts, with no connection to surrounding objects.

# 6. Correcting the Erroneous View of Experience as a Totality

THIS IS THE APPROPRIATE point to address a bias that has persisted since the time of Kant.† It has been absorbed to such a degree into the life of certain circles that it is accepted as truth. Those who presume to question it would be considered superficial and not yet advanced beyond the most elementary concepts of modern philosophy. I refer to the strongly held opinion that the whole perceptual world and its endless multiplicity of colors, forms, tones, and heat is no more than a subjective world of imagination, existing only so long as our senses are open to the influences of a world unknown to us. The whole phenomenal world is interpreted on the basis of this opinion, as a concept within our individual consciousness. Moreover, based on this hypothesis, further assertions are constructed about the nature of cognition. Volkelt, too, has adopted this notion, upon which he bases his epistemology, a masterly production of scientific development. Nevertheless, this is no basic truth, and even less can it be called a high point in the science of knowledge.

We do not wish to be misunderstood under any circumstances. We have no desire to argue (which would be futile) against the contemporary achievements in physiology. However, what may be wholly justified for physiology is certainly not, of necessity, appropriate at the very entry to a theory of knowledge. It may pass as an unassailable physiological truth that the complex of sensations and percepts that we call experience arises first through the cooperation of our physical organism. Yet it remains certain that such knowledge can result only through much reflection and research. This representation—that our phenomenal world is physiologically subjective—is itself a determination of the world reached by thinking; thus it has nothing to do with the initial appearance of this world. This characterization presupposes the application of thinking to experience. It must, therefore, be preceded by an investigation into the interrelationship of these two factors during the act of cognition.

It is presumed that this opinion lifts us above the pre-Kantian credulity, which considered spatial and temporal phenomena as constituting reality, as is still done by the "naïve" person who has no scientific training.

Volkelt asserts:[†] "All acts that call themselves objective cognitions are inseparably bound up with the individual cognizing consciousness; they take place primarily and directly nowhere but within individual consciousness; and they are completely incapable of going beyond the individual or laying hold of or entering the sphere of outer reality."[7] It is, however, impossible for unbiased thinking to discover anything within the form of reality that touches us directly (experience) that could possibly justify us in characterizing it as a mere sequence of mental images. Even a simple reflection—that a "naïve" person, for example, observes nothing in phenomena that could lead to this opinion—teaches us that no compelling reason for such an assumption exists in things themselves. What does a tree or a table contain that would lead me to view it as a mere mental image? At the very least, this view should not be asserted as a self-evident truth.

Volkelt thus entangles himself in a contradiction of his own fundamental principles. We are convinced that he could maintain the nature of experience to be subjective only by disavowing a truth recognized by himself: that experience involves nothing but an unrelated chaos of images without any thinkable meaning. Otherwise, he would have been forced to recognize that, within the world of experience, the cognizing observer is no more relevant than any other object belonging to this observer's realm of experience. However, if one predicates the perceived world as subjective, this is just as much a thought-representation as perceiving a falling stone to be the cause of an impression in the ground. Nonetheless, Volkelt will not acknowledge any interrelationships among the things of experience.

Here lies the inconsistency in his view; he himself disavowed the principle he proclaimed regarding pure experience, thereby enclosing himself within his individuality, no longer capable of emerging. Indeed, he admits this without reservation. Everything beyond the disconnected images of perception remains doubtful for him. According to his view, however, our thinking tries to reach beyond this world of mental images to infer an objective reality, whereas going beyond this world cannot lead to certain, actual truths. All knowledge that we gain through thinking is, according to Volkelt, not protected against doubt. It does not in any way attain the certainty of direct experience, which alone (he claims) provides indubitable knowledge. We have already seen how inadequate it is! But all this arises from the fact that Volkelt attributes a characteristic to sensory reality (experience) that cannot in any way belong to it, and his further assumptions are based on this presupposition.

It has been necessary to give special attention to this writing of Volkelt, because it is the most important contemporary work in this area, and also because it can serve as an example of an effort to reach a theory of knowledge which essentially contradicts the direction of thinking that we represent, based on Goethe's worldview.

## 7. The Experience of Each Individual Reader

WE WANT TO AVOID the fallacy of attributing a characteristic a priori to what is given directly (that is, the first form in which the outer and the inner world appear to us), and refrain from establishing the validity of our reasoning based on that presupposition. Indeed, we determine experience to be precisely a process in which thinking plays no part. There is no question, therefore, of any error in thinking at the outset of our discussion.

It is exactly in this area that a fundamental fallacy arises in many scientific endeavors, especially today—that such scientists imagine that they are reproducing pure experience, though again they are reading out of it only concepts that they themselves have inserted into it. Now it may be argued that we, too, have assigned a number of attributes to pure experience. We described it as endless multiplicity, as an aggregate of unrelated particulars, and so on. Are not these characterizations also made by thinking? Certainly not in the sense that we have used them. We use these concepts only to fix the reader's attention upon reality that is free from thought. We do not wish to attribute these concepts to experience; we employ them only to show the form of reality that is void of any concept.

All scientific inquiries must of course be conducted by the use of language, and language can express only concepts. But there is an essential difference between employing certain words to attribute directly one or another characteristic to something and employing words merely to direct the reader's attention to an object. With the following analogy, we can show that these are two different things. In the first case, A says to B, "Observe that man within his family circle, and you will form an essentially different opinion of him than when you observe his 'official' behavior." It is another situation if A says to B, "That man is an excellent father to his family." In the first instance the attention of B is guided in a certain way, suggesting the judgment of a certain person under certain circumstances. In the second instance, a characteristic is simply attributed to the person, thereby making an assertion. Just as the first case compares with the second, our initial step in this discussion compares with similar phenomena found in other books on this subject. Since the requirements of style, or the way of expressing our thoughts, may at times lend a different appearance to the matter, we wish to declare expressly at this point that our discussion is to be taken only in the sense explained here, and is far from any assertion related to things in themselves.

Now, if we are to have a name for the first way that we observe reality, we really believe that the most adequate term in this case is "appearance to the senses." We understand by the term sense not only the outer senses as mediators of the external world, but also all bodily and mental organs that serve our awareness of the immediate facts. Indeed, the term *inner sense* is usually used in psychology to denote the capacity to perceive inner experiences. The term *appearance*, however, designates merely something perceptible in space or time.

Here we must raise yet another question that will bring us to the second factor that we must consider in relation to the science of cognition, which is thinking. Must we regard the way we come to know experience as something rooted in the nature of things? Is it a characteristic of reality? Much depends on the answer to this question. In other words, if this way of knowing is an essential characteristic of the things of experience—something that belongs to them by their nature in the truest sense of the word—then it is impossible to see how this stage of knowledge can ever be surpassed. We would simply have to make unrelated notes of all that we experience, and such an assemblage of notes would constitute our science. What could all research into the interrelationships of things accomplish if the complete isolation characterizing them in the form of experience represented their real nature?

The situation would be entirely different if, in this form of reality, we worked not with its essential nature, but only with its unessential outer aspect—if we had before us only a shell of the true nature of the world that conceals its essential nature from us and summons us to search further for it. We would then have to try to break through that shell. We would have to begin with this first form of the world in order to master its true characteristics, those essential to its being. We would have to overcome the "appearance to the senses" to develop a higher form of appearance out of it. The answer to this question is given in the following inquiries.

# C : Thought

## 8. Thinking as a Higher Experience within Experience

AMID THE UNRELATED CHAOS of experience (and truly, to begin with, as a fact of experience) we find an element that leads us out beyond this unrelatedness; that element is thinking. Thought, as one fact of experience, already assumes an exceptional position in experience. Regarding the rest of experience, as long as I limit myself to what is immediately present to my senses, I will not get beyond the details.

Imagine that I am facing a liquid that I bring to a boil. First it is still, then I observe bubbles rising, the liquid becomes agitated, and finally steam arises. These form the sequence of individual percepts. No matter how I may twist and turn the thing, if I am limited to what is given by the senses I will discover no interrelationship among those facts. With thinking, however, this is not the case. If I think of causality, for example, the thought's own content leads me to think of effect. I only need to hold the thoughts as they enter direct experience, and already they seem to be lawfully determined.

Regarding the rest of experience, the lawful relationship that must be brought from elsewhere (if it is really applicable to it at all) is present in the very first appearance of the thought. With respect to the rest of experience, what enters as an appearance into my awareness does not immediately manifest the whole of reality; but, in relation to thought, the whole context of the situation is contained entirely in what is given to me. In the first case, I must penetrate the shell to reach the kernel; in the second, shell and kernel are an indivisible unity. It is simply a universal human preconception that thought seems at first to be entirely analogous with the rest of experience. In the case of thought, we merely need to overcome that preconception. With regard to the rest of experience, however, we need to resolve a difficulty which is inherent in the situation itself. *In the case of thinking, what we must seek for along with the rest of experience has itself become direct experience.*

A difficulty is thus resolved that would be difficult to resolve in any other way. It is a justifiable requirement of science that we limit ourselves to experience. However, it is an equally justifiable requirement to look for the intrinsic lawfulness of experience. *Consequently, this intrinsic aspect as such must itself appear some place in experience.* Experience is thus deepened through experience itself. Our epistemology demands experience in the very highest form; it repels any attempt to introduce something external into experience. This theory even finds what is determined by thinking, within experience. Thought manifests in the same way as the rest of the world of experience.

The principle of experience is generally misunderstood, both in scope and in its true significance. In its crudest form, it is the requirement that objects of reality be left as they first appear, and only in this way treated as objects of knowledge. This is purely a principle of methodology; it says nothing about the essence of the experience. If it were asserted that only sensory percepts can become the objects of knowledge (as materialists do), then one could not adhere to this principle. This principle does not determine whether the content is sense-perceptible or an idea. If, in a particular case, it should be applied in the crudest form as mentioned, however, it certainly creates a presupposition. In other words, it demands that objects, as they are experienced, should already have a form suitable to efforts toward knowledge. In terms of experiences of the external senses, as we have seen, this is not the case. It occurs only in thinking. *Only in thinking can the principle of experience be applied in its most extreme meaning.*

This does not exclude the principle from being extended to the rest of the world as well. It possesses other forms besides this most extreme sense. If, for the purpose of scientific explanation, we cannot leave an object just as it is experienced directly, then this explanation can still take place in such a way that the means we employ for this purpose are taken from other areas of experience. We have then not gone beyond the bounds of "experience in general."

A science of knowledge based on Goethe's worldview emphasizes primarily the principle of remaining true to experience. No one has recognized the exclusive validity of this principle so fully as did Goethe. Indeed, he represented that principle just as rigidly as we have demanded here. He would not view all higher perspectives of nature as anything other than experience. They were considered "higher Nature within Nature."[8] In the essay "Nature," he says that we are incapable of getting outside nature. If, therefore, we wish to enlighten ourselves about nature in his sense, we must find the means within nature itself.[†]

But how would it be possible to base a science of knowledge on the principle of experience unless we find the basic element of all that is scientific (ideal conformity to law) somewhere in experience itself? We need merely to grasp this element, as we have seen; we need only submerge ourselves in it, because it exists in experience.

Now, does thought really meet us? Does our individuality become aware of it in such a way that we can justifiably claim for it the characteristics emphasized here? Those who focus on this point will discover an essential difference between the form in which an outer phenomenon of sensory reality becomes known to us (or even some other process of our mental life) and the form in which we become aware of our own thinking. In the first instance, we are aware of being in the presence of a preexistent phenomenon—that is, existent insofar as it has become a phenomenon without our having exerted any determinative influence on its becoming. This is not true of thought. Only in the first moment does thought seem similar to the rest of experience. When we grasp any thought, despite the complete directness with which it enters our consciousness, we know that we are connected directly with its means of becoming. When I have an idea that comes to me suddenly—so that its appearance is, from a certain perspective, much like an external event that must be mediated to me by eye or ear—I nevertheless always know that the thought manifests in the field of my own awareness. I know that my own activity is required before the sudden idea can occur. In the case of every outer object, I am aware that initially it reveals only its exterior to my senses; in terms of thinking, I know with certainty that it reveals its entirety to me, that it enters my awareness as a complete whole. The external stimuli that we must always assume in the case of an outer object are not present in the case of thinking. We must ascribe to these stimuli the fact that sensory phenomena appear to us as preexistent; we must ascribe to them the genesis of those phenomena. In the case of a thought, it is clear to me that this genesis is impossible apart from my own activity. I must work through the thought, recreate its substance, and inwardly live through its smallest details before it can have any importance for me.

Thus far we have arrived at the following facts: When we first contemplate the world, the whole of reality meets us as an unrelated collection, a chaos that includes thought. When we wander through this collection, we find one thing in it that possesses—even in its initial form—the character that the rest of the collection must still achieve, which is thought. What must be overcome in the rest of experience—the form of its immediate appearance—is exactly what needs to be retained in the case of thinking. We find this factor of reality, which must remain in its original state in our consciousness, and we are united with it in such a way that the activity of our own mind is, at the same time, the manifestation of this factor. It is the same thing, viewed from two sides; it is the thought-content of the world. In the one instance, it appears as an activity of our consciousness, and in the other, as the immediate manifestation of conformity to law, complete within itself, a self-determined ideal content. We shall quickly see which side is more important.

Now, because we stand inside the content of thought and permeate it in all its components, we are in a position to know its very nature. The way that it meets us in conformity with lawfulness guarantees that the characteristics we have attributed to it really do belong to it. It can, therefore, serve with certainty as the point of departure for every further way of regarding the world. Its essential nature can be derived from thought itself; if we wish to reach the essential character of everything else, we must begin this inquiry with thinking.

Let us express the matter more clearly. Because we experience a real conformity to law—an ideal determination—only in thinking, conformity to law of the rest of the world, which we do not experience in itself, must be included within thought, as well. In other words, thought and that which appears to the senses confront each other in experience. The latter, however, does not tell us about its own nature, whereas the former tells us about both itself and the nature of what appears to the senses.

# 9. Thinking and Consciousness

HERE, IT MIGHT SEEM as if we ourselves had introduced the subjective element that we were determined to exclude from our theory of knowledge. Even though the rest of the perceptual world is not subjective (as we have explained), thoughts, even according to our own opinion, do have a subjective quality. This argument, however, is based on a confusion of two things: the stage on which our thoughts play their role and the element in which they obtain their content, or inner lawfulness. We really do not produce thought-content in such a way that we determine the interconnections our thoughts will have. We merely bring about the basis of opportunity, so that thought-content can develop according to its intrinsic nature. We grasp thought *a* and thought *b* and offer them an opportunity to enter a lawful relationship by bringing them into mutual contact. It is not our subjective organization that determines this interrelation between *a* and *b*, but the essence of *a* and *b* themselves. The fact that *a* is related to *b* in one way and not another is beyond our slightest influence. Our mind brings about the composition of thought quantities only according to the measure provided by their own content. Thus in thinking we fulfill the principle of experience in its most basic form.

This refutes the opinion of Kant and Schopenhauer and, in a broader sense, that of Fichte—that the laws we create to explain the world are merely a result of our own mental organization, and that we inject them into the world only because of our own thinking.

Another argument might be raised against us from a subjective perspective, as follows. Although the lawful relationship of thought elements does not arise according to the rules of our own organization, but depends on the thought-content itself, nevertheless this very content may be a mere subjective product, a mere quality of the mind, so that we would be merely uniting elements which were first produced by ourselves. In this case, our thought-world would be no more than a subjective appearance. But it is very easy to meet this argument. If it had a solid basis, we would be connecting the content of our thoughts according to laws for which we cannot identify an origin. If such laws do not spring from our subjective being (a supposition we denied just a while ago and that now may be considered as moot), what, then, could provide us with laws of combination for the content we have produced?

Put a different way, our world of thinking is an entity built wholly upon itself; a self-enclosed totality, perfect and complete within itself. Here we see which of the thought-world's two sides is most essential: the objective one of content, and not the subjective one of appearance.

This insight into the purity and perfection of thinking appears most clearly in the scientific system of Hegel. No one else has attributed to thinking a power so complete that it could become the foundation for a worldview out of itself. Hegel has complete confidence in thinking. Indeed, it is the only factor of reality that he trusts in the true sense of the word. Yet, although his point of view is generally correct, he more than anyone else destroyed all respect for thought by the overly crude way that he defended it. The way he presented his view led to the wretched confusion that found its way into our "thinking about thinking." He wanted to make the importance of thought, the idea, evident by describing *rational* necessity to be the same as *factual* necessity. In doing so, he gave rise to the fallacy that thought-judgments are not purely ideas, but factual. His view was soon understood as though he had even looked for thought as if it were a fact in the world of sensory reality. Indeed, he never made himself entirely clear in this regard. It must be firmly understood that the sphere of thought exists only in human consciousness. Then it must be shown that the thought realm does not thus lose any objectivity. Hegel showed only the objective side of thought, whereas most people see only the subjective side, which is seen more easily; and because of this, it seems to them that Hegel treats something that is purely an idea as a *thing*, and hence, mystifies it. Even many scholars today cannot be said to be free of this fallacy. They condemn Hegel because of a defect that he did not possess but only appears to have, because he failed to explain the issue clearly enough.

We acknowledge that our ability to judge faces a difficulty here, but we believe this can be overcome by energetic thinking. Imagine that we actively bring the world of ideas into manifestation and, at the same time, realize that such manifestations are based on their own laws. It is certainly true that we are in the habit of imagining phenomena as though we needed only to stand as passive observers; but this is not an absolute necessity. However odd we may find the idea that we manifest something objective through our own activity—that we not only become *aware* of a phenomenon, but also *produce* it—such an idea is certainly admissible. We need simply to abandon the usual notion that there are as many thought-worlds as there are human individuals—a notion that is no more than an ancient preconception. It is tacitly presumed everywhere without any awareness that another view may be equally valid, and that arguments for the validity of one or the other must at least be considered.

Imagine for a moment that there is really only one thought-content, and that our individual thinking is simply an act of working ourselves, our individual personalities, into the world's thought-center. This is not the place to investigate whether this viewpoint is correct or not, but it is possible; and therefore we have attained what we wished. We have demonstrated that it is quite appropriate to show that the objectivity of thought—which we have declared to be a matter of necessity—is not contradictory in other respects.

From the perspective of objectivity, we may easily compare the work of the thinker to that of a mechanic. Just as a mechanic brings natural forces into reciprocal action and thus brings about a suitable activity and exertion of forces, a thinker causes thought-elements to come into reciprocal activity, and these evolve into the thought-systems that make up our sciences.

There is no better way of illuminating a view than by exposing the fallacies arrayed against it. Here again we will resort to this method, which we have already profitably employed more than once. It is generally presumed that we combine certain concepts into greater complexes, or even think in certain ways, because we feel a certain inner (logical) compulsion to do this. Volkelt also adopted this opinion. But how can this conform to the transparent clarity of the whole thought-world in our consciousness? We know nothing in the world more precisely than we know our thoughts. Why do I need to be compelled if I know the nature of what needs to be combined, and can thus guide myself according to this nature? All the operations of our thinking are processes that occur because of insight into the essential nature of the thoughts, and not according to compulsion. Such compulsion contradicts the nature of thinking.

Yet, although it is the essential nature of thinking to simultaneously impress its content upon its manifestation, it could be that we are unable to perceive this content directly by means of our mental organization. However, this is not the case. The way thought-content meets us guarantees that we have the essential nature of the thing before us. We are certainly aware that, with our mind, we accompany every process in the thought-world. Surely we must believe that the form of a thing's manifestation is determined by its essential nature. How could we reproduce the form of appearance if we did not know the essential nature of the thing? One could certainly think that the form of appearance emerges before us as a complete whole, after which we seek its central core. But it is impossible to maintain the view that we cooperate in producing the appearance without such production arising from the central core of the thing itself.

# 10. The Inner Nature of Thinking

LET US TAKE A STEP closer to thinking. So far, we have considered the place of thinking only in relation to the rest of the world of experience. We have concluded that it holds a privileged position and plays a central role in that world. Now we will turn our attention elsewhere, restricting ourselves to a consideration of the inner nature of thinking. We shall investigate the special nature of the thought-world itself and discover how one thought depends on and relates to another. This is the only way we can answer the question: What, in reality, is cognition? What does it mean to have thoughts about reality? What does it mean to want to explain the world through thinking?

We must keep the mind free of preconceived opinion. Preconception would influence us if we were to assume that a concept (thought) is an image inside of our consciousness, from which we obtain information about an object lying outside. Here, we are not concerned with this or similar assumptions. We take thoughts exactly as we find them. The question of whether they have a relationship to anything else, and of what kind, is precisely what we wish to investigate. Consequently, we must not place it here as our point of departure. This particular opinion about the relationship between concept and object is very common. Indeed, this notion is often defined as the mental counterpart of an object existing outside the mind. Concepts are supposed to reproduce the object, mediating to us its true image. Often, when thinking is the topic of discussion, people imagine only this preconceived relationship. Seldom does anyone attempt to traverse the realm of thought within its own sphere to discover what may be found there.

Here, we will investigate this realm as though nothing existed beyond its boundaries—as if thought were all of reality. Now we turn our attention from the rest of the world.

The fact that Kantian epistemology has neglected this sort of research has been fatal to this realm of science. This omission has directed that science in the exact opposite direction of our own. Owing to its very nature, it is a scientific trend that can never comprehend Goethe. It is not Goethean, in the truest sense of the word, to begin with an assumption that is not based on observation, but one inserted by the observer into the phenomenon. However, this is what happens when one sets, as the peak of scientific knowledge, the view that a presumed relationship exists between thinking and reality, between the idea and the world. The only way to treat this matter in a Goethean way is to enter deeply into the nature of thinking itself and then observe the relationship that arises when this thinking, known according to its own nature, is related to experience.

Goethe always takes the path of experience in the strictest sense. He first takes the objects as they are, then tries to penetrate their nature while completely withholding every subjective opinion. One thus creates the conditions in which the objects can interact, while waiting to see what develops. One tries to allow nature an opportunity to demonstrate her laws under especially characteristic conditions that one brings about.

How does our thinking appear to us when observed as an entity? It is a myriad of thoughts woven and connected organically in the most varied ways. However, once we have penetrated this multiplicity in all directions sufficiently, once again it constitutes a unity, a harmony. All the elements are interrelated and exist for one another; one element modifies the other, restricts it, and so forth. The moment one's mind conceives two corresponding thoughts, it notices immediately that they actually flow into one another to make a unity. It finds, everywhere in its thought-realm, what is interrelated; one concept is connected with another, while a third illuminates or supports the fourth, and so on. Thus, for example, when we find the concept "organism" in our consciousness and then scan our conceptual world, we encounter another concept, "systematic evolution, or growth." It immediately becomes clear that these two concepts belong together and that they merely represent two aspects of one thing. This is true of our whole thought-system. Each individual thought is a part of the greater whole that we refer to as our conceptual world.

When any single thought arises in my consciousness, I cannot rest until it is brought into harmony with the rest of my thinking. I find an isolated concept, apart from the rest of my mental world, completely unbearable. I am simply conscious of the fact that an inwardly established harmony exists among all thoughts and that the thought-world is unitary. For me, therefore, every such singularity is abnormal and false. Once we have struggled through and come to realize that our whole thought-world bears the character of complete inner conformity, we gain the satisfaction our mind longs for; we feel that we have the truth.

While we see truth in the general agreement of all the concepts at our disposal, we are forcefully confronted by the question: "Does thought, apart from all the evident reality of the phenomenal sensory world, have its own content? Once we have removed all sensory content, are we not left with only emptiness, or mere illusion?" It might very well be a widespread opinion that this is true, so we must consider it a little more closely. As we mentioned, it is commonly assumed that the whole system of concepts is nothing but an image of the external world. However, it is firmly maintained that our knowledge evolves in the form of thought—but "strictly scientific knowledge" requires that its content be acquired from without. According to this view, the outer world must provide the substance that flows into our concepts, without which our concepts are empty forms and void of content.[9] If the outer world were to vanish, concepts and ideas would no longer have any meaning, since they exist solely because of that world. This view could be called "negation of the concept," because here the concept no longer has any significance in relation to objectivity; it is merely added to the latter. The world would still exist in all its perfection, even if there were no concepts, for these contribute nothing new to it. They contain nothing that would not be there without them. They exist only because the cognizing subject wants to use them to possess, in a suitable form, what is otherwise already present. They simply mediate nonconceptual content. Such is the point of view under discussion.

If it were well-founded, one of the following three suppositions would have to be correct:

1) The relationship between the conceptual world and the external world consists of the fact that the conceptual world merely reproduces the whole content of the latter in another form. Here, the external world is understood to be the sensory world. If this were the case, one would truly see no need at all to rise above the sensory world, for everything relating and pertaining to knowledge would be given already in this world.

2) The conceptual world takes as its content merely a part of the "appearance to the senses." We may imagine the matter somewhat like this: We make a series of observations of diverse objects. In the process, we discover that certain observed characteristics in one object were previously observed by us. A series of objects pass as in review before our eyes: A, B, C, D, and so on. Suppose A had the characteristics *p q a r*; B shows *i m b n*; C has *k h c g*; and D has *p u a v*. In the case of D, we encounter again the characteristics *a* and *p* observed in A. We designate these characteristics "essential." And, inasmuch as A and D share essential characteristics, we deem them the same type. Thus we unite A and D inasmuch as we maintain their essential characteristics in our thinking. Here we have a thought that does not correspond entirely to the sensory world, and to which the charge of superfluity already mentioned cannot be applied; yet it is no closer to bringing anything new to the sensory world. Against this, we may say first that, before we can determine which characteristics of a thing are essential, we need a certain norm that enables us to distinguish between essential and nonessential. This norm cannot exist in the object itself, since it contains both the essential and the nonessential, inseparably united. This norm should therefore belong to the very content of our own thinking.

Nonetheless, this argument does not completely refute this view, because one could say that it would be unjustified to assume that one characteristic or another is less or more essential to the phenomenon. However, we won't worry about that. It is just a matter of finding the same characteristics in a number of things and then saying they are alike, which is not to say that these same characteristics are also essential. This view, however, does presume something false. As long as we limit ourselves to sensory experience, there is nothing really in common between two things of the same category. An example will clarify this, and the simplest is the best, since it can be observed most easily.

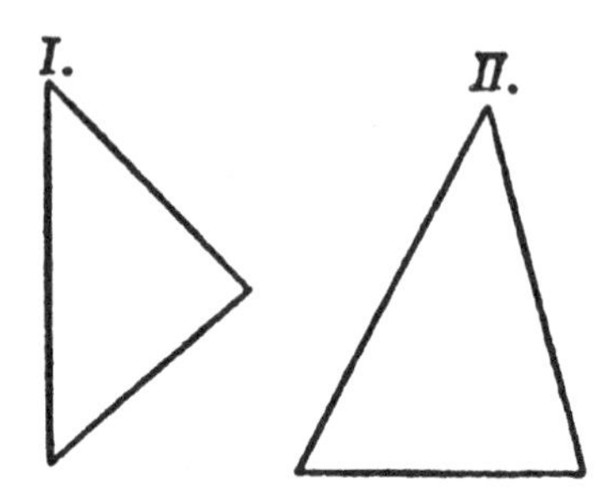


Observe these two triangles. What do they really have in common when we confine ourselves to sensory-experience? Nothing at all. What they have in common is the principle of their formation, which causes them to be classed as *triangles*, and this is attained only when we go beyond the boundary of sensory experience. The concept *triangle* includes all triangles, and we do not arrive at this by observing every *individual* triangle. The concept is always the same, however frequently I may conceive it, whereas I will seldom manage to see two identical triangles. What makes a particular triangle certainly "this" triangle and no other has nothing to do with the concept. A particular triangle is this particular one, not because it corresponds to the concept but because of elements entirely outside the concept, such as the length of its sides, the magnitude of its angles, and its position. Yet, when we see that this essence is not found in any sensory manifestation, it is inadmissible to maintain that the essence of the "triangle" *concept* is borrowed from the outer sensory world.

3. There is also a third possible view. The concept can mediate the apprehension of self-sustaining beings not perceptible to the senses. This would be the nonconceptual content of the conceptual form of our thinking. Those who assume that such beings exist beyond the

limits of experience, while acknowledging the possibility of knowing them, must also see the interpreter of such knowledge in the concept. Later we will clarify the inadequacy of this view. Here we want only to point out that it does not, in any case, contradict the substantial character of the conceptual world. If the objects we think about really are beyond the boundaries of experience and of thinking, then thinking must all the more certainly contain within itself the content upon which it rests. It could certainly not think about objects that have no trace within the thought-world. In any case, it is clear that thought is not an empty vessel; rather, it has content in and of itself, and its content is not equivalent to any other sort of phenomenon.

# D : Knowledge

## 11. Thought and Perception

Knowledge permeates perceived reality with the concepts that our thinking has grasped and worked through. Our mental activity lifts something out of the darkness of mere potential into the light of reality, and through this it supplements and deepens what we passively receive. This assumes that perception must be supplemented by the mind, and thus, that perception is absolutely not definitive, final, and conclusive.

The fundamental fallacy of modern science is that it sees sensory perception as conclusive, or complete. Consequently, the purpose of modern science is simply to record that existence as complete in itself. The only logical view in this sense is positivism, which simply rejects any step beyond perception. Yet, today we observe attempts in virtually all branches of science to see this view as the correct one. In truth, such a requirement would be adequate only for a kind of science that merely enumerates and describes things as they exist among others spatially, and events as they follow one another temporally. The older kind of natural science still comes closest to meeting this requirement. The newer form makes the same demand, for sure, and presents a complete theory of experience; however, the moment it takes the first step into real knowledge, it contradicts that demand.

If we wished to remain with pure experience, we would have to separate completely from our thinking. It degrades thought to deny that thinking has the capacity to perceive within itself entities inaccessible to the senses. Apart from the sensory qualities, another factor must be included within the reality grasped by thinking. Thinking is an organ of the human being intended to observe something higher than what is offered by the senses. Thinking can access a side of reality that is beyond the awareness afforded to a merely sense-bound being. Thought does not exist merely to chew over what the senses reveal, but to penetrate what is hidden from them. Sensory perception provides only one side of reality; the other side is grasped through thinking. Initially, however, thought appears alien to perception, because perception comes into us from outside, whereas thinking works outward from within us. The substance of our thinking appears as an inwardly complete organism; everything is strictly connected. Individual members of the thought-system determine one another; ultimately, each concept has its roots in the totality of our thought structure.

At first glance, it seems as though the inner freedom from contradiction in thought—its self-sufficiency—would make any transition to the percept impossible. If the thought-characterizations could be satisfied in only one way, thinking would actually be confined within itself—we would be unable to emerge from within it. But this is not the case. The representations are such that they may be satisfied in a variety of ways; however, the element that produces this variety of ways must not be sought within thinking itself. Consider a thought-representation: "The Earth attracts every other body." We soon see that the thought allows for the possibility of its being fulfilled in diverse ways, but thinking can no longer reach those ways. Here, there is room for another element—sensory perception—that provides a form of specialized thought-representations, which they themselves leave open. The world meets us in this specialization when we utilize mere experience. Psychologically, in fact, the derivative comes first.

In every scientific approach to reality, this is the process: We encounter a concrete percept, which confronts us as a question. An impulse arises within us to investigate its true nature, which the percept itself does not convey. That impulse is simply the upward activity of a concept from the darkness of our consciousness. We then hold this concept firmly as the sense percept goes along in parallel with the thought process. The mute percept suddenly speaks an intelligible language, and we realize that the percept is seeking the concept we have grasped. Thus, a judgment has occurred, which is different from the form of judgment that unites two concepts without reference to percepts. When I say: "Freedom is a being's own determination from within," I have also formed a judgment. The constituents of this judgment are concepts not given to me by perception. The inner unity of our thought (which we dealt with in the preceding chapter) is based on such judgments.

The subject of the judgment we will now consider is a percept, and its predicate is a concept—for example, "The animal before me is a dog." In such a judgment, a percept is inserted into my thought-system at a certain place. Let us call this kind of judgment perceptual. Through perceptual judgment, we know that a certain sense-perceptible object, by its nature, corresponds to a certain concept. Therefore, before we can comprehend what we perceive, we must have already pictured the percept inwardly as a determinate concept. Any object not processed in this way would be unintelligible to us.

We see this truth best through the fact that those who have lived a rich mental life also penetrate far more deeply into the experiential world than do those whose mental life is shallow. Much that would go by the latter without leaving a trace instead leaves a deep impression upon those with a rich thought life. ("If the eye were not sun-like, it could never see the sun.")[†] One could ask, however: Do we not encounter countless phenomena in life of which we have not previously conceived? Further, do we not form concepts of such things on the spot? Undoubtedly we do, but is the sum of all potential concepts equal to those I have formed in life thus far? Is my conceptual system incapable of evolving? In the presence of a reality unintelligible to me, am I not able to activate my thinking so that it develops, immediately, the concept I need to match the object? I need only the capacity of drawing a determinate concept out of the store of the thought-world. I did not consciously know this particular concept previously in my life, but I can draw such a concept from the world of thoughts accessible to me. Where and when I grasp the concept is not important to its content. Indeed, I produce thought-characterizations out of the thought-world. Nothing flows from the sensible object into that content. In the sensed object, I simply recognize the thought that I draw from within myself. Certainly, this object inpels me at a certain moment to invoke only this particular thought-content from the unity of all potential thoughts, but it certainly does not furnish me with the material for constructing the thought. This I must draw from within myself. Only when we activate our thinking does reality attain to true characterizations. Previously mute, reality now speaks a clear language. Our thinking is the interpreter that explains to us the silent gestures of experience.

People are accustomed to viewing the conceptual world as void of content and, by contrast, generally see the percept as filled with content and thoroughly determinate—to the degree that it becomes difficult for the facts of a situation to assume their proper place. One completely ignores the fact that mere perceiving is the emptiest thing imaginable, and that perception receives all of its content from thinking. The sole truth of the matter is that perception holds the constant flow of thought in a definite form, without our active cooperation. The fact that one who has a rich mental life sees a thousand things that may remain unseen by one who is mentally impoverished shows as clearly as sunlight that the substance of reality only reflects the content of the mind, and that we receive only an empty form from outside. Of course, we must have the inner power to recognize ourselves as the creator of this content, otherwise we will only ever see the reflection, and never our own reflected mind. Indeed, if we are to recognize ourselves in the reflection of a mirror, we must first know ourselves as individual personalities.

All sensory perception eventually resolves itself, in terms of its essential nature, into ideal content. Only then does it appear transparent and clear to us. The sciences are largely unaffected by any awareness of this fact. One instead considers thought-determinations to be the characteristics of objects, such as colors, odors, and so on. Thus, it is supposed that all bodies are described by the attribute they possess while in their current state—resting or moving—until an external influence alters this state. It is in this form that the law of inertia plays a role in natural science. However, the actual situation is quite different. In my conceptual system, the concept "body" exists in many modifications. One of these is the thought of a thing that can move itself or come to rest. Another is the concept of a body whose condition changes only through external influences; this latter modification I designate "inorganic." If, therefore, I encounter a body that, in the percept, reflects this conceptual definition, I designate it as inorganic and connect it with all determinations that follow from the concept of an inorganic body.

All sciences should be permeated by the conviction that their content is solely thought-content, and that their only relationship to perception is that they see a particular form of the concept in the perceived object.

# 12. Intellect and Reason

THINKING MUST FULFILL a twofold purpose: First, to form sharply outlined concepts; second, to unite individual concepts into a unified whole. The first is a process of differentiating; the second, one of combining. These two mental tendencies certainly do not enjoy equal favor in the sciences. The number of people who can discriminate between even the minutest trifles is noticeably greater than the number of those who possess a unifying power of thinking that penetrates to the depth of matters.

For a long time, the purpose of science was supposed to involve mainly the precise differentiation of phenomena. Just recall the state of natural science that confronted Goethe. Through the influence of Linnaeus, the ideal of this science had become the investigation of precise differences among individual plants so that their most insignificant characteristics could be used to establish new classes and sub-classes. Two species of animals or plants differing only in the most nonessential details were thus assigned to different classes. If some creature had been assigned to a certain class but was found to show an unexpected divergence from the arbitrarily determined class character, it was considered unimportant how this divergence might be explained by the nature of that character itself; one simply established a new class.

Such differentiation is the work of the intellect; it needs only to divide, and base concepts on those divisions. This stage is a prerequisite to all higher forms of scientific knowledge. Above all, we must have fixed and sharply outlined concepts before we can look for a harmony among them. Moreover, we must not stop at the stage of division. To the intellect, cause and effect are divided; as are mechanism and organism, freedom and necessity, idea and reality, spirit and nature, and so on. All of these distinctions are established by the intellect. They must be established; otherwise the world would appear blurred, obscure, and chaotic. It would form only a unity, because for us it would appear completely vague. Conversely, intellect alone is incapable of going beyond this process of analysis; it merely clings to the separated members.

The purpose of reason is to go beyond this stage. It must allow the concepts of the intellect to intermingle. It must show the real inner unity of all that the intellect keeps strictly separated. This separation is introduced artificially; it is a necessary point of passage for knowledge, but not its conclusion. Those who apprehend reality only in an intellectual way alienate themselves from it. In place of reality, which is actually a unity, they establish an arbitrary multiplicity, or diversity, which has nothing to do with the essential nature of reality.

This is the source of discord between intellectually-pursued knowledge and the human heart. The thinking of many people is not developed enough to reach a unified worldview that they can grasp with complete conceptual clarity, but they may be quite capable of penetrating the inner harmony of the world through their feeling. The heart gives them what a trained scientist receives through reason. When such people encounter an intellectual worldview, they scornfully reject the endless multiplicity and cling to the unity, which they do not really know but sense more or less vividly. They see very well that the intellect is alienated from nature and that it loses sight of the spiritual bond that unites the parts of reality.

Reason leads us back to reality. Reason knows completely the unity of all being, which previously had been felt or only vaguely suspected. The intellectual view must be deepened by the faculty of reason. If the intellectual view is seen as an end in itself instead of as a necessary stage, it yields not reality but only a caricature of it. It is sometimes difficult to connect thoughts formed by the intellect, and the history of science provides considerable evidence of this fact. We often see the human mind struggling to reunite the differences created by the intellect. In the reasoned worldview, one eventually reaches an undivided unity.

Kant pointed out the difference between intellect and reason.[†] Reason, he said, is the capacity to perceive ideas, whereas the intellect is limited to seeing the world divided, with its parts in isolation. Reason is indeed the capacity to perceive ideas. Here we must define the difference between *concept* and *idea*, which we have ignored thus far. For our purpose, until now we needed only to discover the qualities of thought that are present in both concept and idea.

A concept is a single thought grasped by the intellect. When I bring a number of such single thoughts into a living flow, so that they intermingle and become connected, thought-structures arise that exist only in reason and cannot be attained by the intellect. Creations of the intellect surrender their separate existence to reason and live on only as parts of a totality. The structures formed by reason we shall call *ideas*.

Kant stated that the idea reduces a multiplicity of intellectual concepts to a unity. However, he described the structures that manifest through reason as mere fantasy, or illusions,[†] with which the human mind deludes itself, because it is always trying to realize a unity of experience that is never given to it. Unities formed in ideas are not, according to Kant, based on objective conditions; they do not flow from the thing itself, but are mere subjective norms by which we bring order into our knowledge. Kant, therefore, designated ideas not as constitutive principles that would have to be determinative, but as regulative principles that have meaning and significance only for our systems of organizing knowledge. However, if we observe the way in which ideas come into existence, this view is shown immediately to be false. Of course, subjective reason[10] needs unity, but such need lacks any content; it is merely an empty effort toward synthesis. When confronted by something lacking any intrinsic unity, reason cannot, out of itself, produce unity. When confronted by a multiplicity that can be harmonized, however, reason can form harmony. Such multiplicity is the world of intellectually formed concepts.

Reason does not presuppose any particular wholeness, but rather an empty form of synthesis; reason is the capacity to reveal harmony when it exists in the object itself. Concepts themselves are synthesized by reason to form ideas. Reason reveals the higher wholeness of intellectual concepts—the unity that the intellect possesses in its image, but lacks the capacity to see. The fact that this is overlooked leads to much misunderstanding in the application of reason in the various areas of scientific knowledge. To some degree, every science, and even ordinary thinking, must begin with reason. If we unite the subject-concept with the predicate-concept in the theorem "Every object possesses weight," we have united two concepts and thus have the simplest activity of reason. Wholeness, as the object of reason, is present prior to any thinking or use of reason; nonetheless, it is hidden and exists only as potential, not as an actuality. The human mind then introduces analysis, allowing us to have complete insight into reality through the rational synthesis of the separated members.

Anyone who does not accept this presupposition must either view all thought-combinations as the arbitrary work of a subjective mind, or assume that a unity exists behind the world we experience which, in some unknown way, forces us to reduce the multiplicity again to a whole. In this case, we combine thoughts without insight into the true reasons behind the connection we make. Thus, we do not recognize truth; rather it is forced upon us externally. All knowledge arising from such a presupposition would be called dogma. We will return to this later.

Every such scientific viewpoint will encounter difficulties when asked to explain why we bring about some combination of thoughts. In other words, this view requires us to look for subjective reasons for combining objects whose objective interrelationship is concealed from us. Why would I form a judgment if the thing requiring the connection of subject-concept and predicate-concept is unrelated to the formation of such a judgment? Kant took this question as the starting point for his critical work. At the beginning of his *Critique of Pure Reason*, we find this question: How are synthetic judgments possible a priori? That is, how is it possible for me to unite two concepts (subject and predicate) if the content of one is not already contained in the other, and if the judgment is not a merely experiential judgment, the establishment of a single fact? Kant considers such judgments possible only when experience depends on the presupposition of their validity. Thus the possibility of experience is the determining factor if we wish to form such a judgment. The judgment has validity only if I can say that experience is impossible unless one or another synthetic judgment is a self-evident fact. But this principle cannot be applied to ideas themselves. According to Kant, ideas do not have even that degree of objectivity.

Kant finds that the theorems of mathematics and pure natural science are such valid propositions a priori. He takes, for example, the theorem 7 + 5 = 12. Kant concludes that the sum twelve is by no means already contained in the sequence of seven plus five. I must go beyond seven plus five and call upon my viewpoint, and then I find the concept *twelve*. My point of view requires a mental picture of the proposition 7 + 5 = 12. Objects of experience, however, must approach me through the medium of my viewpoint, and thus accommodate themselves to its principles. Such propositions must be true before experience is possible.

When judged objectively, this whole arbitrary thought-structure of Kant fails to stand up. It is impossible that I would have absolutely no clue of the subject-concept that leads me to the predicate-concept. Both concepts are reached through the intellect in relation to something that is itself whole. Let no one make a mistake in this regard. The mathematical unit that is the basis of number is not primary; rather, the primary thing is the magnitude, which is a certain number of repetitions of the unit. I must presume a magnitude when I speak of a unit. The unit is an image created by the intellect, which separates it from a whole just as it separates effect from cause, substances from their attributes, and so forth. When I think *seven plus five*, I actually hold twelve mathematical units in mind—not as a whole, but separated into two parts. If I think of the sum of the mathematical units united, then this is really the same thing. This identity I express in the opinion 7 + 5 = 12. This is also true of the geometrical examples that Kant cited. A limited straight line with endpoints A and B is an indivisible unit. My intellect can form two concepts of this; it may consider the straight line as a direction or as the path between points A and B. Out of this arises the judgment, "The shortest distance between two points is a straight line."

Inasmuch as the members that enter the judgment are concepts, all judgments are simply the reunification of what the intellect has divided. The interconnection comes to light as soon as one enters the content of the intellectual concepts.

## 13. The Act of Cognition

REALITY REVEALS ITSELF to us in the two separate spheres of experience and thought. Experience must be considered in two ways: First, to the extent that the whole of reality, apart from thinking, has a form of manifestation that must appear in the form of experience; second, to the extent that it is inherent in the nature of the human mind (whose essential nature consists in observation, or outwardly-directed activity) that the objects to be observed must enter its field of vision—that is, the objects must again be given to the mind in the form of experience. It may be that this form of what is given does not contain the essential nature of the thing, in which case the thing itself requires that it first appear in perception (in experience), and only later reveal its essential nature to the mental activity that goes beyond perception. Another possibility is that the essential nature may be present in what is given directly, though we cannot be aware of this essential nature because of the second circumstance—the mind's requirement that everything appear before it as experience. The second possibility is true of thought; the first is true of all other reality. In the case of thought, it is necessary only to overcome one's subjective biases in order to grasp this in its innermost essence. In the case of all other reality, what rests upon the actual situation in objective perception—that the immediate form of appearance must be overcome in order to explain it—rests, in the case of thought, only upon a peculiarity of our minds. In the former case, the thing itself gives itself experiential form; in the latter, an experiential form arises from the organization of our mind. In the former case, we do not yet have the whole when we comprehend the experience; in the latter case, we do have it.

This is the basis for the dualistic notion that we must overcome knowledge, thinking, cognition. People find themselves confronted by two worlds, whose interrelationship they must bring about. One is experience, which we know contains only one half of reality; the other is thought: self-complete, and into which that external experiential reality must flow before a satisfying worldview can come about. If the world were populated entirely by merely sense-bound creatures, its essential nature (its ideal content) would remain hidden forever; although laws would control the world processes, those laws would never become apparent. Before these laws can be made apparent, there must be, between the law and its form of manifestation, a being who not only has the organs needed to perceive the sensory form of reality dependent upon the laws, but also has the capacity to perceive the lawfulness itself. Both the sensory world itself and the ideal nature of this world must come to meet this being, who must unite the two factors of reality by means of reasoning activity.

Here it must be obvious that our mind should not be regarded as a receptacle for the world of ideas containing the thoughts within itself, but as an organ that perceives those thoughts. The mind is no less an organ of apprehension than are the eyes and the ears. Thought is related to our mind as light is related to the eye and sound to the ear. Surely, no one would think of color as something that permanently impresses itself on the eye, remaining there as if it adhered to it. Nonetheless, this is the prevailing view when it comes to the mind. It is presumed that a thought of each thing forms itself in the consciousness and remains there to be brought forth as needed. One particular theory has been based upon this view, as if thoughts we are unaware of at the moment were preserved in our minds, lying just below the threshold of consciousness.

These strange opinions dissolve into nothing when we recall that the world of ideas is self determined. What does this self-determined content have to do with the multiplicity of consciousness? One would hardly suppose that it determines itself within indeterminate multiplicity in such a way that one partial content is always independent of the other! The matter is perfectly clear; the content of thought is such that it requires only a mental organ for its manifestation, whereas the number of beings possessing such an organ is unimportant. Therefore, an indefinite number of beings endowed with minds may be confronted by a single thought-content. The mind thus perceives the thought-content of the world like an organ of comprehension. There is only a single thought-content of the world. Human consciousness does not constitute the ability to produce thoughts and store them up, as is generally believed, but rather the ability to perceive thoughts (*ideas*). Goethe expressed this excellently: "The idea is eternal and unique;† the fact that we also use the plural is unfortunate. All things that enter our awareness and discussions are simply manifestations of the idea; we express concepts, and to that extent the idea itself is a concept."

Living in these two worlds, that of the senses and that of thoughts—with one pressing in from below and the other shining down from above—human beings become masters of knowledge and thus unite the two into an undivided whole. From one perspective, the outer form calls to us, from the other, the inner being calls, and we must unite the two. Here our epistemology has lifted itself above the views usually adopted by similar inquiries, which never get beyond formalities. It is said, "Knowing is the elaboration of experience," without determining exactly what is elaborated. The matter is defined by saying that, in cognition, perception flows into thinking, or that thinking, by virtue of a certain inner compulsion, advances from experience to the real entity behind it. But these are all mere formalities.

An epistemology that tries to understand the important role of cognition in the world must first declare its ideal purpose. This involves offering a solution to unresolved experience by revealing its central core. Such a science must then determine the nature and content of that central core. It is thought, or *the idea*. Finally, it must show how to uncover the core. Chapter 11, "Thinking and Perception," explains this. Our epistemology leads to the positive conclusion that *thought* is the essential nature of the world, and that individual human thinking is its particular form of manifestation. A mere formal theory of knowledge cannot do this, but remains barren. It has no opinion on the relationship between what knowledge attains and the nature and activity of the world. And yet this relationship must be found in a theory of knowledge. Surely this science must show us where our knowledge is going to take us and, therefore, where all other sciences will lead us.

Only through an epistemology can we attain the view that thought is the central core of the world, because such a science shows the connection between thought and the rest of reality. Without a science that focuses its investigations on this relationship, how could we come to understand the relationship between thinking and experience? Moreover, how could we ever know that a certain spiritual or sensible entity is the elemental force of the world if we did not investigate its relationship to reality? Therefore, the discovery of the essential nature of a thing will always involve a return to the world's content of ideas. If we wish to stay with clear definitions and not grope around in uncertainties, we must not step outside the domain of this content. Thought is a whole in itself; it is self-sufficient and may not pass beyond itself without entering a void. In other words, it must not, when trying to explain something, resort to things not found within itself. Something that thought could not encompass would be an absurdity. Everything is resolved in thought and eventually finds its place there.

In terms of our individual consciousness, this means that, if we wish to establish anything scientifically, we must limit ourselves completely to what is given to us in consciousness. The error of believing that human knowledge is limited arises when we realize that we cannot skip over our own consciousness without finding ourselves in unreality, but do not also perceive that the essential nature of things exists within our consciousness in the act of perceiving ideas. If we cannot go beyond our consciousness, and if the essential nature of reality is not within consciousness, then we can never find our way to that essential nature. Our thinking is then bound to this one side, and knows nothing of what is beyond it. According to our point of view, however, such an opinion is simply thinking that misunderstands itself. Limits to knowledge would be possible only if external experience itself forced us to inquire into its nature and determined the questions we asked about it. But this is not the case. The need arises in thinking to hold up its own essential nature to experience, as it perceives this experience. Thinking can have only a definite tendency to see its own lawfulness in the rest of the world, but never anything of which thinking is ignorant.

Another fallacy must also be rectified at this point—the belief that thinking is insufficient to constitute the world, as if something else (force, will, or whatever) must be added to the capacity of thinking in order to render the world possible. As soon as we reflect sufficiently, however, we see that all such factors actually amount to nothing but abstractions drawn from the perceptual world, which must themselves wait to be explained by thought. Other than thought, every component of the world would require a form of apprehension, or cognition, other than thought. These other components we would have to apprehend in ways other than through thought; after all, thinking yields only thoughts. However, we already contradict ourselves if we want to explain the roles of these other components in the activity of the world, and thus must resort to concepts for this explanation. Moreover, apart from sensory perception and thought, there is no third capacity given to us. And we cannot consider any part of sensory perception to be the core of the world, since closer inspection of all its constituents shows that, as such, they do not contain its essential nature. This essential nature can, therefore, be found exclusively in thought.

## 14. Cognition and the Ultimate Ground of Things

KANT TOOK A GREAT STEP forward in philosophy by directing humanity's attention toward the individual self. We must seek the reasons for the certainty of our postulates by using the capacities of our own minds, and not through truths forced upon us from without. "In science, be convinced only through yourself." This is the slogan of the Kantian philosophy. This is why he specifically called it a *critical* philosophy, in distinction from the sort of dogmatic philosophy that maintains and then tries to prove preconceived postulates. Here, an antithesis arises between two scientific trends, but Kant did not address it with the acumen he displayed otherwise.

Let us now fix clearly in mind how a scientific postulate comes into existence. It unites two things, either a concept and a percept or two concepts. The second sort includes, for example, the postulate "no effect without a cause." It may be that the objective reasons why the two concepts flow together is beyond what they themselves contain, which is all that is given to me. I may then still have all sorts of formal reasons (freedom from contradiction, certain axioms) that lead me to a particular combination of thoughts. But these reasons have no influence upon the thing itself. The postulate is therefore based on something I can never reach objectively. Consequently, a real insight into the thing is impossible for me; I know about it only as one standing outside it. What this postulate expresses is in a world unknown to me; only the postulate itself is in my own world. This is the nature of dogma.

There are two sorts of dogma: the dogma of revelation and that of experience. The first gives us, in one way or another, truths about things that are beyond the reach of our vision. We possess no insight into the world from which these postulates spring. We must believe in their truth, and cannot get at the underlying reasons. For experiential dogmas, the case is similar. If we believe that we should simply limit ourselves to pure experience, and are able to observe only its variations without penetrating to a knowledge of the causative forces underlying them, we make assertions about a world whose basis is inaccessible to us. Here, too, truth is not gained through understanding the inner functioning of the phenomenon; rather, it is imposed externally on the thing itself. Whereas earlier science was dominated by the dogmas of revelation, contemporary science suffers from dogmas of experience.

Our view of the matter has shown that to presume a fundamental source of being outside of the idea is absurd. The whole source of being has poured itself out into the world; it has merged with the world. It reveals itself in its most perfect form in thought, just as it is in itself. Consequently, if thinking makes a connection or a judgment, it is the essence of the ground of the world itself, poured into thought, that unites with it. In thought, we are not given postulates about any ground of the world in the beyond; its very substance has flowed into it. We have a direct insight into the objective, not merely the formal, grounds for the formation of a judgment. A judgment is made about its own content, not about something alien. Therefore, our view forms a basis for real knowledge. Our epistemology is truly critical. According to our view, not only is nothing conceded to revelation, for which thinking does not contain objective reasons, but experience must also be perceived within thinking—not just in terms of its manifestation, but also its effects. Through thinking, we lift ourselves from perceiving reality as a product to perceiving reality as something that produces.

The essential nature of a thing thus comes to light only in relation to the human being. The essential being of each thing appears only for human beings. This forms the basis for relativism as a worldview; a trend of thought which assumes that we see all things in the light that the human being lends to them. This view also bears the name anthropomorphism, which has many representatives. Most of these, however, believe that this peculiarity of our cognition alienates us from objectivity as it is, in and of itself. We perceive everything, so they believe, through the spectacles of subjectivity. Our worldview shows us the exact opposite. If we want to reach the essential nature of things, we must view them through these spectacles. The world is not merely known to us as it appears, but rather appears as it is, though only to contemplative thinking. The form of reality that the human being in this way delineates through scientific knowledge is ultimately its true form.

Now we must extend the epistemology we consider correct—the one that leads to the essential being of reality—into the individual areas of reality. We will now show how the true nature of experience can be found in its individual forms.

# E : Knowing Nature

## 15. Inorganic Nature

The simplest form of action in nature seems to us to be the one in which an event results entirely from factors external to one another. Here, an event or a relationship between two objects is not determined by an entity that manifests itself in the outer forms of appearance—that is, an individuality that expresses its capacities and character through outward activity. The occurrence or relationship has been brought about only because something happens that produces a certain effect on something else, thus passing its own condition to another thing. The conditions of one thing appear as a consequence of those of another. We use the term *inorganic nature* for the system of activities that occurs in this way, where one fact is always the result of other similar such facts.

Here, the process or typical relationship depends on outer conditions, and the facts bear distinguishing traits of those conditions. If we change the way that the external factors come together, the result of their coincident existence will, of course, also be changed; the phenomenon thus brought about is altered. What is the nature of this coincident existence in the case of inorganic nature as it comes into our direct field of observation? It bears the trait we call *direct experience*; we have a particular example of the "experience in general," which depends on the interrelationships of sense perceptible facts. However, it is precisely these connections that appear unclear or opaque in our experience. One fact confronts us, but at the same time so do numerous others. As we survey the multiplicity before us, we are uncertain about which of these other facts have closer, and which more remote, relationships to the fact we are considering. Some may be required for the very occurrence of the event, while others may simply modify it; without the latter, the event would likely occur, though in some other form.

With this, we are shown the path that cognition must take in this area. If we are not satisfied with the combination of facts in our immediate experience, then we must move on to a different combination that satisfies our need for an explanation. We need to create conditions such that an event will appear to us in transparent clarity, as the necessary result of those conditions.

Let us recall the exact reason that thought already contains its nature in direct experience. It is because we stand within, not outside of, the process which creates thought-associations from individual thought-elements. Thus, we are given not only the finished result of the process, but also the activity of that process. When we confront any occurrence in the outer world, it is important to first perceive the impelling forces that bring it from the world-center to the periphery. A lack of transparency and clarity regarding any phenomenon or relationship in the sensory world cannot be overcome unless we see with precision that it is the result of a particular constellation of factors. We must know that the process we see arises through the cooperation of this and that element of the sensory world. Then our intellect must be able to understand completely the mode of activity in this interaction. The facts must be related in an ideal way that is suited to our minds. Of course, things will function according to their own qualities in the relationships our intellect creates for them.

We see immediately what we gain in this way. If I look randomly at the sensory world, I see processes caused by the interaction of so many factors that it becomes impossible to see directly which causes are actually behind various effects. I observe an event and, at the same time, facts *a, b, c,* and *d.* How can I distinguish immediately which of these facts participate, and to what degree, in the process? It becomes transparent when I first investigate which of the four facts is absolutely necessary to the process. I find, for example, that *a* and *c* are absolutely necessary. Then I find that the process would occur without *d,* but with important differences. Moreover, I see that *b* is not essential and could be replaced by another factor. In the following diagram, figure 1 symbolizes the constellation of elements strictly regarding sensory perception; figure 2 symbolizes this constellation for the mind. The mind thus groups the facts of the inorganic world in such a way that it sees the consequence of the conditions of facts in the form of a process, or relationship. Thus the mind introduces the element of necessity into the realm of chance.

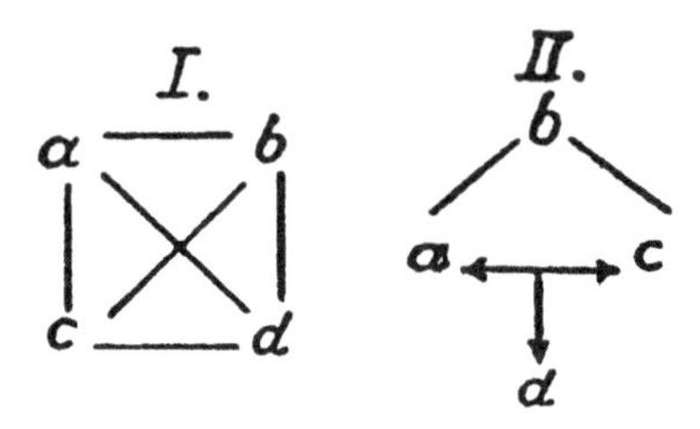


Some examples will make this clear. If I am confronted by triangle *ABC*, I do not see directly that the sum of the three angles always equals 180 degrees. This does not become clear until I group the facts as follows:

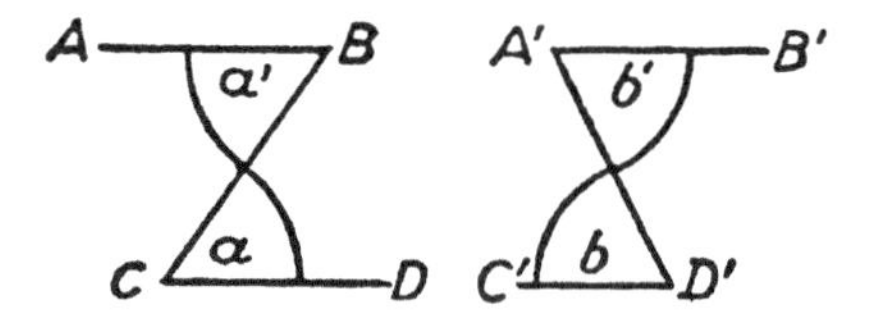


In the following illustrations it becomes clear immediately that angle *a*' equals angle *a* and that angle *b*' equals angle *b*. (*AB* and *CD* are parallel to *A*'*B*' and *C*'*D*' respectively.) If, in triangle *ABC*, I draw a line through apex *C* parallel to base *AB*, I find again that angle *a*' equals angle *a* and that *b*' equals *b*.

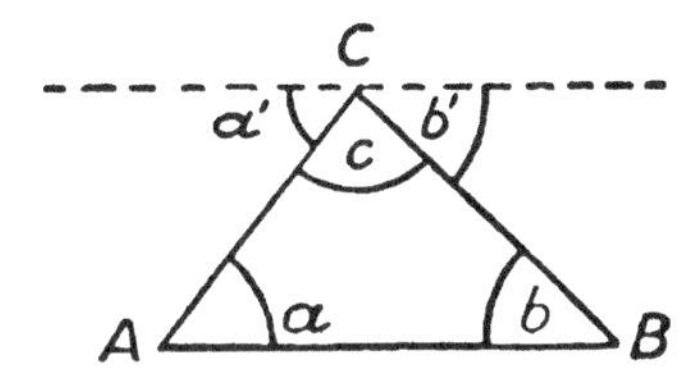


Now, because *c* equals itself, then together the three angles of the triangle must equal 180 degrees. Here, I have explained a complex combination of facts by reducing it to simple facts, and given the circumstances presented to the mind, the corresponding relationship follows necessarily from the given facts.

Another example is as follows: I throw a stone in a horizontal direction. The trajectory of this stone is represented by the line *ll'*. When assessing the driving forces that come into consideration here, I find 1) the propelling force exerted, 2) the force with which the Earth attracts the stone, and 3) the force of atmospheric resistance.

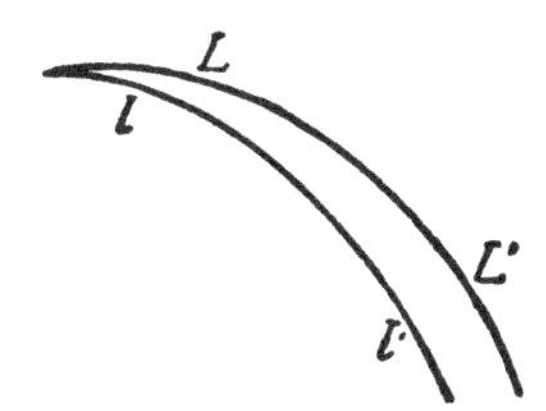


If I examine this situation more closely, I find that the first two forces are essential to the particular character of the path, whereas the third is subordinate. If only the first two forces were present, the stone would follow the path *LL'*. I find this to be true if I ignore the third force and consider only the first two. To actually do this is neither possible nor necessary; I cannot eliminate all atmospheric resistance. But for my purpose, I need only apprehend in thought the nature of the first two forces and bring them into the necessary relationship, deducing path *LL'* as the necessary result of this interaction. *In this way, the mind resolves all phenomena of the inorganic world into those of a form in which it appears that the effect seems to come directly and necessarily from the causative factor.*

After arriving at the law of the stone's movement resulting from the interaction of the first two forces, if we then also apply the third force to it, the result is path *ll'*. Additional conditions might complicate the matter even more. Every composite occurrence in the sensory world appears as a web of simple facts that the mind can penetrate and simplify.

Now, an *elemental phenomenon*, or basic fact, is what one calls a phenomenon in which the process flows in a transparently clear way, directly from the factors under consideration. An elemental phenomenon is identical with an objective law of nature, because it expresses the fact that an event took place under certain specific conditions, as well as the fact that it *had* to happen. We realize that the event had to happen owing to the very nature of the phenomena considered. The general requirement for external empiricism arises from the belief that any accepted fact which goes beyond what we derive empirically leaves us groping in uncertainty. We realize here that we can remain completely within the phenomena and still achieve knowledge of what is necessary to its occurrence. Today's highly esteemed inductive method can never do this. Basically, it proceeds in this way: It observes a phenomenon that arises through certain means and conditions. Then it observes the same phenomenon happening a second time under similar conditions, from which it concludes that a general law exists that dictates the requirements for this occurrence. It then pronounces this finding as a law.

Such a method remains entirely external to the phenomena; it does not penetrate deeply enough. Such laws are generalized from separate facts, and must await confirmation of the rule through those individual facts. Our method knows that such laws are simply facts torn from the confusion of chance, and called necessary. We know that a specific effect must appear when factors *a* and *b* are present. We do not go beyond the phenomena. The essence of knowing, as we view it, is simply perceiving what has happened objectively. The only difference is in the way we group the facts. Nevertheless, as a result of this difference, we penetrate a step closer to objectivity than experience allows. We combine the facts so that they act according to their own natures and *only* thus; and in such a way that their activity is not modified by extraneous circumstances.

We attach the greatest importance to the fact that these assertions can be justified wherever we perceive the real functioning of science. Only erroneous opinions concerning the scope and nature of scientific principles contradict them. Whereas many of our contemporaries confront contradiction when they enter the field of practical research, the harmony between our assertions and all true research can be easily shown in every instance.

Our theory demands a definite form for every natural law. It presupposes a combination of facts and maintains that, whenever such a combination actually occurs, a certain event must take place. Every natural law, therefore, has this form: When particular facts interact, a certain phenomenon arises. It would be easy to show that all natural laws exhibit the form seen in the following examples: When two bodies of unequal temperature are in contact, heat passes from the warmer into the less warm until the temperature of the two are equal. If a fluid is contained in two connected vessels, the levels equalize in the two vessels. If a body stands between a source of light and another body, it casts a shadow upon the second body. In mathematics, physics, and mechanics, anything that is not a mere description must be an elemental phenomenon.

All advances in knowledge rest upon the perception of elemental phenomena. When we are able to separate an event from its relationship to other events and explain it as the effect of certain elements of experience, then we penetrate a step deeper into the world's processes.

We saw that the elemental phenomenon yields itself purely to thinking if the relevant factors are brought together in thought in accordance with their true nature. However, one can also artificially manufacture the necessary conditions; this happens in scientific endeavors. In this way, we can control the occurrence of certain factors. Naturally, we cannot ignore all related circumstances, but there is a way to get around them by manufacturing a phenomenon with modifications. We allow first one and then another contributing circumstance to work. We then discover that one constant persists through all of these modifications, retaining what is essential to all the combinations. This is the *higher experience* within experience. It is the *basic fact, or elemental phenomenon.* The purpose of the experiment is to insure that nothing affects a given process in addition to what we have included in our calculation. We arrange certain conditions whose nature is known to us, and observe what follows. Thus, we have an objective phenomenon resulting from subjective creation. We have something objective that is also thoroughly subjective. *The experiment, therefore, is the true mediator between subject and object in inorganic science.*

We find the seed of this view, as we have developed it, in the letters that Goethe and Schiller exchanged. From the beginning of 1789, their letters were concerned with this. They call this method *rational empiricism,*[†] because it accepts only objective occurrences into the content of knowledge; while the web of conditions (or laws) which our mind discovers in them holds those objective occurrences together. Rational empiricism comprises sense-perceptible phenomena, connected in a way that only thought can grasp. One will see the consistent result of this theory by comparing these letters with Goethe's essay, "The Experiment as Mediator between Subject and Object" (*Der Versuch als Vermittler von Subjekt und Objekt*).[11]

Thus, the general relationship we have determined between experience and knowledge is always valid in inorganic nature. Ordinary experience is only one half of reality; to the senses, only this half is present. The other half is present only to our ability to see with the mind. The mind raises the experience from a mere "appearance for the senses," to a thought-form compatible with itself. We have shown how it is possible in this area to rise from effect to cause. The mind achieves the latter when it confronts the former.

An opinion will give us scientific satisfaction only when it introduces us to a final wholeness. However, at no point does the inorganic aspect of the sensory world appear whole; nowhere does an individual whole arise. A process only points to another upon which it depends, this to a third, and so on. Where does it end? The sensory world in its inorganic aspect does not reach individuality. Only as a whole is it complete. To have a whole, we must therefore strive to understand, as a whole, the inorganic world as a system. Such a system is the cosmos.

A thorough understanding of the cosmos is the goal and ideal of inorganic natural science. Any scientific endeavor that does not penetrate this far is no more than a preparation; it is one part, but not the whole itself.

# 16. Organic Nature

For a long time, science was held back when confronted by organic nature. Science considered its methods inadequate to comprehend life and its manifestations. It believed that the laws applicable to inorganic nature no longer exist for organic nature. Science simply denied that it could understand the organic world as it did the inorganic—that we can understand the phenomena if we know its preconditions. The assumption was that a creator designed organisms purposefully according to a specific plan, and that the purpose of each organ was predetermined; thus, all inquiry should concern itself only with the functions of organs: Why is this or that one present? Inquiry into the inorganic world meant examining the prior circumstances of a phenomenon, whereas science considered those conditions unimportant to the facts of life; the primary concern was the *purpose* of that phenomenon. Likewise, questions about the processes that accompany life did not focus on the natural causes, as it had in the case of physical manifestations; rather, it was simply thought that such processes should be attributed to a special capacity for life. Such a force was thought to produce the organism, and this belief simply took precedence over other natural laws. Until the beginning of the nineteenth century, science just did not know how to approach organisms; it was limited to the inorganic world.

By looking for the laws that govern organisms in the thought of the Creator rather than in the objects themselves, science cut itself off from any possibility of achieving an explanation. How can a thought come to me? I am limited to what I have before me; if it does not itself disclose its laws to my thoughts, my knowledge reaches an end. In science, it cannot be a matter of divining the plans of some being standing outside of the events themselves.

At the close of the eighteenth century, the view that still prevailed was that no science could explain the phenomena of life in the same way that, say, physics serves to explain things. Indeed, Kant even sought to give a philosophic basis for this view;† he believed that the human intellect must progress from the particular to the general. The specifics, or particulars, are given to the intellect, and from these the mind abstracts general laws. Kant called this form of thinking *discursive*, and he considered it the only form available to human beings. According to his opinion, therefore, science must approach phenomena in a way such that the particular, in and of itself, is without a concept, but only later summarized under an abstract concept. In the case of organisms, Kant did not find that this condition could be fulfilled. In this case, the individual organism reveals an arrangement of *meaning*, or a concept; the particular shows traces of the concept in itself. However, according to the Königsberg philosopher, we lack any capacity to understand such an entity. We cannot understand it unless we can separate the concept from the individual organism, where one represents the general, the other the particular. Nothing remains, therefore, except to make the *idea of purpose* the basis for observing organisms; one approaches living creatures with the assumption that the basis of their manifestation is systematic intention. Thus, Kant placed the lack of science, as it were, on a scientific basis.

Goethe firmly protested against such an unscientific approach. He was never able to see why our thinking would be inadequate to investigate the origin of a creature's organ, instead of merely its purpose. It was in his nature, as an ever-present urge, to regard every entity in terms of its inner perfection. It seemed unscientific to him to be concerned only with the outer function of an organ, observing only its usefulness to something else. What does this have to do with the inner, essential nature of a thing? He was never concerned with the use of something; rather, he always wished to know how it evolves.† He wished to observe an object not as finished, but as becoming, so that he might know its source. Goethe was attracted especially to Spinoza,† for whom the external purpose of organs and organisms was unimportant. For knowledge of the organic world, Goethe demanded a method just as scientific as one we apply to the inorganic world.

Without his ingenious approach, yet just as urgently, the need arose repeatedly for just such a method in natural science. Today, few scientists doubt the possibility. Of course, it is another question whether scattered attempts to introduce such a method have been successful. Most importantly, a great error has been committed in this regard. It was believed that one should simply take the methods of inorganic science into the organic realm. In general, only the methods applied by inorganic science were considered scientific; people thought that, if an organic science is possible, it must be "scientific" in the same way as, say, physics. However, one forgot that the nature of an organic science might be far broader than "an interpretation of the universe according to the laws of the physical world." Even today, we have not yet recognized this truth. Rather than investigating what makes the inorganic sciences "scientific," and then looking for a way to apply that to the living world while maintaining its organic requirements, the laws discovered at those lower stages of existence are simply declared universal.

Above all, we should investigate the foundation of scientific thinking, which we have done in our discussion. In the preceding chapter, we recognized that inorganic lawfulness is not the only such type, but rather a particular instance of all possible conformities to law. The method of physics is merely one particular instance of a general scientific method, in which consideration is given to the nature of the object under examination and to the field served by this science. If we extend this method to the organic, we eliminate the specific character of the latter. Instead of investigating organic nature according to its own qualities, we force an alien law upon it. By thus denying the organic, we can never understand it. This scientific approach simply repeats on a higher level what it gained on a lower one and, in doing so, expects to bring the higher form of existence under these ready-made laws used elsewhere. Thus, the higher form eludes our efforts to investigate, since we do not know how to handle it according to its own nature.

All this arises from the erroneous opinion that scientific method is independent from the objects under investigation; *our* laws define scientific method, not those of the objects under investigation.

We believe that we must think about objects—indeed, the whole universe—in the same way. We intend for our investigations to show that, by the nature of our minds, we must think inductively, deductively, and the like. In all this, however, we ignore the fact that the objects of science may not be able to bear the methods of observation to which we subject them.

When we consider the views of Haeckel, surely the most important of contemporary scientific theorists, we can justify the reproach which we have made about today's organic natural science—that it has not carried over the principles of scientific observation in general, but only those of inorganic nature. Haeckel's intention is clear in his demand[†] that all scientific efforts "should validate the causal interconnection of all phenomena."[12] It is also clear in his statement: "If the mechanics of the soul were not so infinitely complicated, and if we were able to fully survey the historic evolution of the soul's functions, we could reduce them all to a mathematical formula of the soul."[†] His intention is to deal with the entire world according to the stereotyped pattern of the physical sciences.

This requirement is basic, as well, in contemporary Darwinism (though not in its original form). We have seen that the explanation of a process in inorganic nature intends to show its lawful derivation from other sense-perceptible realities—to deduce it from other objects that belong likewise to the sensory world. Nevertheless, how does contemporary "organic science" apply those principles of adaptation and the survival of the fittest (neither of which we should dismiss as having a basis in fact)? Does one subscribe to the belief that we can deduce the nature of a certain species from its environment, just as we might deduce the warming of a body from the sunlight falling on it? One forgets entirely that we can never prove that such conditions gave rise to that nature in its significant features.

Outer conditions may have a determining influence, but they are not a creative *cause*. It is surely safe to say that, under given circumstances, a species must so evolve to develop this or that organ in a special way; but its essential quality, the specific organic character, cannot be deduced from external conditions. Suppose that an organic entity has the essential characteristics *abc*; it then evolves within certain external influences so that its characteristics have assumed the form *a'b'c'*. When we consider these influences, we understand that *a* has evolved into the form *a'* ; *b* into *b'* ; *c* into *c'*. However, the specific nature of *abc* can never be shown to result from external influences.

Above all, we must direct our thought to this question: Where do we find the content of a general class in the particular case of a single organic entity? We know quite well that specialization arises from external influences, but we must derive the specialized form itself from an inner principle. Why one particular form evolves becomes clear when we study the environment of an entity. Yet, surely, that special form is something in and of itself; we see that it possesses certain characteristics. We see what is essential to it. A self-formed content complements the outer manifestation; it tells us what we need in order to derive those characteristics. In inorganic nature, we become aware of a certain fact, and we look for a second and third fact to explain it, with the result that the first fact seems to be the necessary result of the latter ones. This is not the case in the organic world, where we need something in addition to the facts. We must find a basis for the influences coming from outer circumstances; yet one that does not passively allow itself to be determined by them, but instead actively determines itself under their influence.

What is this fundamental basis? It must be what appears in the particular with the form of the general. Nevertheless, a definite organism always appears in the particular. Thus, the basic element is an organism in the form of the general—a general image of the organism that includes all of its particular forms within itself. Following Goethe's precedent, we shall call this general organism the *type*. Regardless of what the word *type* means etymologically, we use it in the Goethean sense to mean simply what we have described. The type is not developed in all its perfection in any one organism. Only rational thought can comprehend this type by abstracting it as a general image from the phenomena. The type is thus the *idea* of the organism—animal nature in the animal and the general plant in the particular one.

We must not imagine anything fixed under this term *type*. It is completely unrelated to what Agassiz (Darwin's most notable adversary) called "an embodied creative idea of God."† The type is a fluid concept, from which we may derive all of the particular species and families, which we consider subtypes, or specialized types. The type does not exclude the theory of descent. It does not contradict the fact that organic forms evolve one from another. It is only the rational protest against the idea that organic evolution involves only successively appearing, actual (sense-perceptible) forms. It is basic to this whole process of evolution, establishing the interconnections in all of its infinite multiplicity. The type is the inner aspect of what we experience as the outer forms of living creatures. Darwin's theory presupposes the type.

The type is the true elemental organism—the elemental plant or animal according to how it ideally specializes itself. It cannot be any single sensorially existing entity. What Haeckel or other naturalists see as the elemental form is already a particular one; it is merely the simplest form of the type. The fact that temporally it appears first in the simplest form does not mean that later forms are necessarily the results of preceding forms. All forms show themselves to be results of the type; both the first and the last are its manifestations. We must take this type as the basis for true organics, rather than simply trying to derive the single species of animals or plants from one another. Like a red thread, the type manifests through all of the evolutionary stages of the organic world. We must grasp it firmly and wander with it through this great, variegated kingdom. In this way, it becomes intelligible; otherwise, like the rest of experience, it disintegrates into a mass of unrelated particulars. Indeed, we deceive ourselves even when we believe that we have reduced the later, more complex forms to the earlier, simpler form, and that in the latter we have the original one; in reality, we merely derive one specialized form from another.

Friedrich Theodor Vischer[†] once opined that Darwin's theory would require a revision of our concept of time. Here, we reach a point where it becomes clear in what sense such a revision would have to occur. It would have to show that deducing a later thing from an earlier one is not an explanation, and that the first in time is not the first in principle. Every derivation must arise from what constitutes the principle; at most, we would need to show the factors that led one kind of entity to evolve before another.

In the organic world, the type plays the same role that natural law plays in the inorganic world. Just as natural law allows us to recognize each individual event as part of a whole, the type allows us to view a single organism as a specific version of the elemental form.

We pointed out that the type is not an isolated, crystallized conceptual form, but rather, it is fluid; it can assume a myriad of forms. The number of these forms is endless, because what makes the elemental form into a particular specialized one does not affect the elemental form. It is no different from the way a natural law controls innumerable single manifestations, because the particular determining factors that appear in these single instances have nothing to do with that law. However, what we are dealing with is essentially different from inorganic nature, where it is a matter of showing that a certain sense-perceptible fact can appear one way and not another, owing to the existence of a certain natural law. The fact and the law confront each other as separate factors; when we observe a fact, the only mental work required is to recall the relevant law. It is different in the case of a living entity and its manifestations; there, it is a matter of evolving the particular form that we experience from the type, which we must have determined. The mental process we must perform is essentially different; we do not simply fix the type as something finished, like a natural law, in contrast to the particular manifestation.

It is a definite, fixed, and final law that every entity, unless prevented by subordinate circumstances, falls to the Earth in such a way that the distances covered in successive intervals of time are in the ratio 1:3:5:7.... This elemental phenomenon takes place whenever two masses (the Earth and bodies thereon) come into a reciprocal relationship. If a specific case enters our field of observation, in which this law applies, we need only to connect the sensorially observable facts with those stated by the law, and we shall find the law confirmed. We treat the particular case according to the law. The natural law expresses the interrelationship of the individual facts of the sensory world, but as such, it continues to be valid in relation to particular phenomena. In the case of the type, we must evolve the particular case that meets us out of the elemental form. We must not compare the single forms with the type to see how the type governs the single form; rather, we must let the forms arise from the type. Natural law governs a manifestation as something standing above it; the type flows into the individual living entity, and identifies itself with it.

Thus, if a science of organics sets out to be scientific in the sense that physics or mechanics is scientific, it must show the type as the most general form, and then also in various ideal separate forms. Mechanics, too, groups various natural laws so that the actual conditions are always assumed hypothetically. It must be the same in organics. Here, too, if we wish to have a rational science, we must presuppose hypothetically determined forms that the type takes on. One would then have to show how one can always reduce these hypothetical forms to a definite observable form. Just as we trace a phenomenon in the inorganic world to a law, in the organic world we evolve a specific form from the elemental one. Organic science does not arise through the external comparison of the specific and the general, but through the evolution of one form out of another. Mechanics is a system of natural laws, and likewise organics must be a succession of forms evolved from the type. In the former case, however, we bring together the single laws and arrange them into a whole, whereas here we must let the single forms arise in a living way from one another.

At this point, one might raise an argument: If the type is altogether fluid, how is it possible to set up a chain of special types arrayed together as the content of organic science? One could easily imagine that, in each special instance observed, a particular form of the type is to be recognized, yet we cannot simply assemble such actually observed instances in the name of science. However, we can do something else; we can allow the type to follow its course through the series of possibilities, and then in each case fix (hypothetically) one or another form. In this way, we arrive at a series of forms, deduced by thought from the type, as the content of a rational organic science.

An organic science is possible that will be just as scientific, in the strictest sense, as mechanics. The only difference is the method. Proof is the method of mechanics, and each proof depends on a specific rule. There are always certain assumptions (i.e., conditions accessible to experience are given), and we can determine what occurs when these assumptions are correct. We then comprehend a particular phenomenon based on the law. We think, *Under these conditions, the phenomenon occurs; the conditions are present, therefore, the phenomenon must occur.* This is the thought-process we use to explain an event of the inorganic world when we meet it. This is the method of proof. It is scientific because it permeates a process completely with the concept—because it brings together perception and thinking.

However, we cannot use this method of proof in organic science. The type does not require, under certain conditions, a definite phenomenon to take place; it does not determine anything regarding a relationship between mutually alien elements that confront one another. It determines only the conformity to law of its own parts. It does not point beyond itself, like a natural law. The particular organic forms can evolve only from the universal type-form, and the organic entities that we experience must coincide with one of these derivative forms of the type. Here the evolutionary method must replace the method of proof. We do not establish that the external conditions act upon one another in a certain way, thus bringing about a certain result; rather, we develop a particular form out of the type, under certain external conditions. This is the radical difference between the inorganic and organic sciences. No other method of research makes this distinction as consistently as did the research method of Goethe. No one else recognized, as Goethe did, that an organic science must be possible apart from any vague mysticism or teleology, and without assuming particular ideas about creation. In addition, no one else more definitely rejected the demand to begin applying the methods of inorganic science to this field.

The type, as we have seen, is a more complete scientific form than the elemental phenomenon. Moreover, it presumes a more intensive mental activity than that required by inorganic science. In reflecting on the processes of inorganic nature, our sensory perception provides us with the content. Here it is our sensory organization that yields what we grasp only with the mind in organic science. Awareness of sweetness, sourness, warmth, cold, light, color, and so on requires only healthy senses. There, thinking discovers only the form of the matter. The type, however, intimately connects content to form. Thus, the type does not determine the content only in a formal way, as does the law; rather, it permeates the content in a living way from within, as its very own. Our mind confronts the task of cooperating productively in creating the content along with its formal aspects. The mode of thinking in which the formal aspects and the content are connected directly has always been called *intuition.*

Intuition appears repeatedly as a scientific principle. The English philosopher Reid describes intuition† as the activity of being convinced of the actual existence of an outer phenomenon at the same time that we perceive it (through sensory impressions). Jacobi thought that our feeling of God gives us not only the feeling, but also supports the *existence* of God.† We can see that the nature of intuition always gives more than the content itself; one knows through the way one thinks (without proof), merely through direct conviction. We consider it unnecessary to prove such thought-representations in relation to what we perceive, and believe that we possess them in unity with the content.

With the type, however, this is actually the case. Consequently, it cannot provide any means of proof, but merely suggests the possibility of developing each special form out of itself. For this reason, the mind must work far more intensely in apprehending the type than in grasping the natural law. It must create the content with the form. It must act in the way that the senses do in inorganic science, which we call intuitive perception (*Anschauung*). The mind itself, therefore, must be perceptive on this higher plane. Our power of judgment must perceive in a thinking way, and think in a perceiving way.† Goethe [in his essay "The Experiment as Mediator between Subject and Object"] was the first to explain what we are describing as an intuitive power of judgment. He pointed out, as a necessary form of apprehension in the human mind, what Kant wanted to prove we are unable to attain because of the nature of our whole constitution.

In organic nature, the type replaces the role played by natural law (the elemental phenomenon) in the consideration of inorganic nature; similarly, intuition (judgment with perception) replaces the power of judgment through proof (judgment with reflection). One believed that we could apply to organic nature the same laws that are used at a lower stage of knowledge; likewise, one believed that we could apply the same methods in both areas of investigation. Both suppositions are wrong.

Science has frequently treated intuition with considerable contempt. The fact that Goethe expected to reach scientific truths by means of intuition was considered a defect in his thinking. Of course, when intuition leads to a scientific discovery, many people consider its results to be very important. One then hears that a chance idea often carries one farther than trained methodical thought does. Indeed, people frequently call it intuition when one reaches a truth by chance—a truth that researchers must use roundabout means to prove. Nevertheless, people generally deny that intuition itself can be a principle of science. To have scientific value, anything that intuition happens upon must then be proven (so it is thought). Thus, Goethe's scientific achievements have been seen as brilliant chance ideas to be confirmed later by the strict methods of science.

For organic science, however, intuition is the correct method. Our exposition makes it quite clear that Goethe's mind found the right way in organic science by depending on intuition. The method appropriate to organics harmonized with the very constitution of his mind. Consequently, it became even clearer to him to what extent organics differs from inorganic science; one became clear to him in relation to the other. This is why he was also able to outline with precision the essential nature of the inorganic.

Science attaches such little value to intuition largely because its achievements supposedly do not deserve the degree of credibility we give to scientific achievements based on proof. Frequently, one refers only to what has been proved as knowledge; everything else is called belief. One must consider that intuition means something different for *our* scientific way, which is convinced that we grasp the core of the world in thinking—a meaning very different from the one granted it by the worldview that shifts the core reality into a realm unavailable to our research.

We must regard the method of proof as a meagre compensation for our lack of insight into the real nature of things, so long as we can perceive no more than a reflection of their essence in the world (insofar as we either experience this world or penetrate it through thought)—

that is, so long as we can see no more than an alien, unknown, yet active image, that remains hidden behind this veil, both at first glance and to all scientific research. Because, under these conditions, we would not realize that a thought-connection arises from the essential content given in the thoughts themselves—and therefore through the thing itself—we would have to think that we could support such a connection only because it harmonizes with certain essential convictions (axioms), so simple that they are neither susceptible to, nor in need of, proof. If, then, a scientific postulate were offered without proof—even one that in its whole nature excludes the method of proof—this would seem to have been forced on us externally. A truth would appear to us and we would not recognize the foundation for its validity. We would not think it possible to have any knowledge or insight into the thing; we would instead have to believe that the reason for its validity is beyond the reach of thought.

Our worldview is not in danger of believing that the limits of proof are also the limits of scientific knowledge. It has led us to the view that the core of the world flows into our thinking. We do not merely think *about* the nature of the world; rather, thinking flows together *with* the nature of reality. Intuition does not impose a truth on us externally; from our perspective, outside and inside do not exist as they do in the beliefs of the science we have described, which is the opposite of our own. For us, intuition is a direct experience of being within, or penetrating into, the truth, upon which we are then given everything related to it. The truth merges completely with what our intuitive judgment gives us. We do not find the essential characteristic of belief in this—that we gain the final truth but not the reasons for it, and that we lack a penetrating understanding of the phenomenon. Insight gained through intuition is no less scientific than that gained by proof.

Every individual organism is an arrangement of the type in a specialized form. The individual regulates and determines itself outwardly from a center. It is wholly complete in itself, which is true only of the cosmos in inorganic nature. The ideal of inorganic science is to grasp the wholeness of all phenomena as a unified system, so that we may recognize each phenomenon consciously as an element of the cosmos. In organic science, by contrast, the ideal is to have the greatest possible perfection of the type in its phenomenal forms, which we see evolving in a series of separate entities. The important thing is to return to the type through all of its manifestations. In inorganic science, we have the system; in organic science, the activities of comparing each form with the type.

Spectral analysis and improvements in astronomy extend the truths attained on Earth into the universe. In this way, those sciences approach the first ideal. We will fulfill the second ideal when science fully recognizes Goethe's comparative method.

# F : The Humanities

## 17. Introduction: Mind and Nature

We have exhausted the realm knowing nature, and organics is the highest form of natural science. Higher yet are the spiritual, or cultural, sciences, which require an essentially different attitude of mind toward the subject than that required of us toward the natural sciences. In the natural sciences, the mind plays a universal role. Its purpose, as it were, is to bring the world process itself to a conclusion. What exists without the mind is only one half of reality—incomplete and, at every point, a mere fragment. There the mind must evoke into phenomenal existence the innermost impelling forces of reality, even though these would nevertheless possess validity without its subjective intervention. If human beings were mere sensory beings without mental capacities, inorganic nature would depend no less upon natural laws; however, they would never manifest themselves as such. Of course, beings would exist to perceive the outcome (the sensory world), but never could they perceive what created it (the inner lawfulness). In fact, the genuine, truest form of nature is expressed in the human mind, whereas only nature's outer aspect would exist for a mere sensory being. Science here plays a significant role in the world; it finishes the work of creation. Nature is interpreted to itself in human consciousness. Thought is the final member in the sequence of processes that forms nature.

This is not so in the humanities, where human consciousness deals with mental content itself—with the individual human mind, with the creations of culture, of literature, with the succession of scientific convictions, with the creations of art. The mind grasps the mind. Here reality already has in itself the ideal, or lawfulness, which otherwise appears only in mental comprehension. What the natural sciences offer as a product of reflecting about the objects, is inherent in them in this case. Science therefore plays a different role; the essential being would also be present here in the objects even without scientific efforts. Here, we work with human actions, creations, and ideas. Humanity is in discourse with itself. This science has a different mission to discharge than when confronting nature. Here again, the mission first appears as a human need. The necessity of finding the idea inherent in nature, as well as its reality, first appears as a need of the mind; likewise, the purpose of the humanities exists first as a human impulse. Again, it is only an objective fact announcing itself as a subjective need.

The human being should not, like a being of inorganic nature, act upon another being according to external norms and according to laws that control externally. Nor should the human being be only a single form of a general type; as human beings, we should intrinsically prescribe our own purpose, the goal of our existence and of our activity. If a person's actions are the results of laws, these laws must be self-created. The intrinsic nature of a person, among peers, in a state, and in history, must not be formed by external determinations. *Human beings must be self-determined.* How we fit into the texture of the world depends upon our own activity. Human beings must find the place for participation in the world's machinery. This is the purpose of the humanities. Human beings must know the world of mind, so as to participate in the world in accordance with that knowledge. Here is the source of the mission of psychology, sociology, and the science of history.

It is inherent in nature that law and activity fall apart, and that the former appears to control the latter. Conversely, it is the essential nature of human freedom that the two coincide; that human activity expresses itself directly in its effect, and therefore that the outcome is self-determined. The humanities, therefore, are the sciences of freedom in the highest sense. The idea of freedom must be the essential point and dominant idea in this realm. This is why Schiller's letters on aesthetics rank so highly; they attempt to discover the nature of beauty in the idea of freedom, because freedom is the principle that permeates what is beautiful. The mind occupies only the place in the universal wholeness of the world that it gives to itself as an individual.

In organics, we must keep in mind the general, or the idea of the *type*. In the humanities, however, we must take hold of the idea of *personal existence*. The point here is not the idea as it lives in the general (or type), but as it appears in the single being (or individual). It is, of course, not important how personal existence evolves particular forms out of itself and initially manifests in sense-perceptible existence; the important thing is *personal existence as such*, self-enclosed and self-directed.

The type must realize itself in the individual being. The destiny of the human being is to achieve, as an ideal, a truly self-sustaining existence. It is entirely different to speak of a general humanity and a general natural law. In the latter case, the particular arises from the general; in the idea of humanity, the general arises from the particular. If we are able to discern general laws of history, they are laws only inasmuch as historical personalities have established them as goals or ideals. This is the inner contrast between nature and mind. Nature requires knowledge that ascends from the directly given as *the caused*, to what the mind can grasp as *the cause*. Mind requires knowledge that proceeds from perceiving the given as the cause, to perceiving it instead as the caused. In the humanities, the particular establishes the laws; in the natural sciences, the general provides the laws.

The sole interest in the humanities—the *particular*—has value for the natural sciences only as a transitional point. In the humanities, we consider the *general*—what we seek in the natural sciences—only to the extent that it illuminates the particular for us. It would go against the spirit of science if, with regard to nature, we were to limit ourselves to the immediate experience of the particular. However, it would also be fatal to the mind if we tried to comprehend Greek history, for example, in a general scheme of concepts. In the former case, the mind, cleaving to the phenomenal, would gain no knowledge; in the latter, the mind, proceeding according to a general pattern, would lose its sense for the individual.

# 18. Psychological Cognition

THE FIRST SCIENCE in which the mind deals with itself is psychology; here the mind observes itself, face to face. Fichte assigned an existence to human individuals only to the extent that they ascribe this existence to themselves.† In other words, the human personality has only the traits, characteristics, and capacities that it ascribes to itself through insight into its own being. A person would not recognize his or her possession of an unknown human capacity, but would attribute it to someone else. Fichte was wrong to suppose that he could base all knowledge of the universe on this truth. Nevertheless, it is destined to become the highest principle of psychology, whose method it determines. If the human mind possesses a characteristic only to the degree that it attributes this to itself, then the psychological method involves the mind being absorbed in its own activity. Thus, this method is self-apprehension.

Of course, we are not limiting psychology to a science of the characteristics of any individual human being. We instead separate the individual mind from its accidental limitations and unimportant traits, and try to lift ourselves to a consideration of human individuality in general. Indeed, it is not important that we consider the wholly chance individual, but that we become clear about the self-determining individual in general. Anyone who might want to say at this point that we should then be dealing only with the *type* of humanity confuses the type with the generalized concept. It is essential to the type that it stands as the universal in contrast to its single forms. This is not essential to the concept of the human individual. Here the universal acts directly in the individual being, but this activity expresses itself in various ways according to the object toward which it directs itself. The type exists in single forms and, as such, comes into reciprocal activity with the external world. The human mind has only one form. Nevertheless, certain objects move one's feelings, or an ideal inspires one to act, and so on. We must not deal with a particular form of the human mind, but always the entire and complete human being. We must release the human mind from its surroundings in order to apprehend it. If we wish to arrive at the type, we must ascend from the single form to the elemental form; if we wish to arrive at the human mind, we must ignore its expressions or particular acts, observing it in and of itself. We must discover how it behaves in general, not how it has behaved in some particular situation. In the case of the type, we must separate the universal form from the single forms; in psychology, we must separate the single form only from its surroundings.

For psychology, it is no longer the case, as it is in organics, that we recognize in the particular being the formation of the general, or elemental, form. In perceiving the single forms, we recognize the elemental form itself. The human mind is not *one* expression of its ideal, but its *exact* expression. Jacobi is mistaken to believe that when we become aware of our inner being we also perceive that a uniform nature is its basis (intuitive self-apprehension);[†] in actual fact, we become aware of this uniform nature itself. In this way, what is otherwise intuition becomes self-contemplation. This is also essentially a necessity with regard to the highest form of being. The highest form of content that the human mind can attain is what it can read out of phenomena. If it then reflects upon itself, it must recognize itself as the direct manifestation of this highest form, even as its vessel. What the mind finds as unity in multiform reality, it must find in its own individuality as direct existence. What the mind contrasts as the general with the particular, it also attributes to its own individuality in its essential nature.

From all this, it becomes clear that we cannot develop genuine psychology unless we penetrate the nature of the human mind through its own activity. In place of this method, the subject of psychology today has not been the human mind itself, but the *appearances* through which the mind expresses itself. It is supposed that the mind's isolated outer expressions can be related externally, just as we relate the facts of inorganic nature. In this way, we try to establish a "theory of the soul without soul."[†] Our reflections make it clear that, by using such a method, we lose sight of the most important thing. We should loosen the human mind from its outer manifestations, and instead recognize it as their source. Psychologists restrict themselves to outer manifestations and lose sight of the mind. In this way, they have also allowed themselves to arrive at a mistaken view that would apply the methods of mechanics, physics, and such, to all sciences.

We experience the soul as such, just as we do its single actions. Everyone is aware of the fact that our "I" gives rise to our thinking, feeling, and willing. Every activity of our personality relates to this center of our being. If we ignore this union with personality in any activity, then the activity ceases to be a manifestation of the soul. It then falls into the category of either inorganic or organic nature. If two balls lie on a table, and I knock one against the other, all that happens is resolved into a physical or physiological event, so long as we ignore my intent and will. In all manifestations of the human mind—thinking, feeling, and willing—the point is to recognize these in their essential nature as expressions of the personality. This is the basis of psychology.

However, human beings are not just self-contained, but they also belong to a society. The activities and achievements of both oneself and one's folk-group are made manifest in the individual. The individual mission of each human being also fulfills the mission of that person's larger community. The important thing is that the position of each person within the community allows the power of that individual to develop its full effectiveness. This is not possible unless the social group is the kind in which each human being can find an appropriate place to work, and finding such a place must not be left to chance.

Determining how the individual lives within a community is a matter for sociology and political science, as the social group is the subject of these sciences. They must show what form the organism of the state must assume if the spirit of the community is to be expressed within it. The constitution that a group provides for itself must be developed out of its innermost nature. Here, too, significant fallacies exist. One does not tend to regard political science as an experiential science.

It is believed that the constitution of every group of people can be determined according to a certain template.

In truth, the constitution of a people is simply its individual character, firmly established as forms of law. Those who would indicate the direction of a society's activity must refrain from imposing anything externally; the direction should simply express the unconscious character of the people. As Goethe says, "It is not the intelligent person who rules, but intelligence; not the rational person, but reason."†

To understand the spirit of a community to be rational is the method of sociology. Humanity belongs to a whole, whose nature involves the organization of reason. Here, too, we may cite Goethe: "The rational world is to be conceived as a great, immortal individual who continually brings into being what is needed, and in this way even becomes the master over chance."† Psychology investigates the nature of the single individual; likewise, sociology (the psychology of community spirit) must investigate that "immortal individuality."

# 19. Human Freedom

THE WAY WE VIEW the sources of our knowledge cannot help but influence the way we view our everyday activities. People act according to the influences on thinking that lie within the individual. People direct their activities according to self-initiated purposes and goals. Nevertheless, it is clear that such goals, purposes, and ideals will bear the character that shapes the rest of one's world of thought. Thus, dogmatic science will give us a practical truth which is essentially different from what our epistemology provides. If the truths one acquires through science arise from an objective necessity outside of thought, then those ideals that serve as the foundation of one's conduct will be no different. Here, one acts according to externally established laws, which provide a behavioral norm prescribed externally to that person. Nevertheless, this is the character of a commandment that humanity must obey; dogma as a practical truth is a moral commandment.

The foundation of our theory of knowledge is entirely different. Our theory holds that the only foundation for facts is the thought-content residing within them. Therefore, when a moral ideal arises, it is the inner power in its content that governs our conduct. We do not conduct ourselves according to an ideal given as a law, but according to the ideal, by virtue of its content, that is active within us. The motive for action is not outside, but within us. If we felt controlled by a sense of duty, we would be compelled to act in a specific way, because it commands us to do so; *compulsion* would come before *will*. This is not valid according to our view. The human will is sovereign and performs only what lies in the human personality as thought-content. The human being does not accept laws from an external power; rather, the individual creates them.

According to our worldview, who, in fact, should give these laws to individuals? The world-foundation has poured itself completely into the world.† It did not remain outside of the world in order to control it externally; it has not withheld itself from the world, but impels everything internally. Its highest form of appearance in the reality of ordinary life is thought and, with it, the human personality. If, therefore, the ground of the world has goals, they are identical with the goals that the human spirit sets for itself in life. We are not acting according to the purposes of the guiding power of the world when we search out one of the commandments of this power; rather, when we act according to our own individual insights, the guiding power of the world manifests in them. This guiding power does not live somewhere outside of humanity as will; rather, it has entirely renounced its own will so that everything depends on human will. Before we can create our own laws, we must abandon all concern about such matters as universal determinations that come beyond the human world.

We take this opportunity to point out the excellent treatment of this subject by Kreyenbuhl† in *Philosophical Monthly* (*Philosophische Monatshefte*, vol. 18, no. 3). This paper correctly explains how the fundamental principles of our conduct always arise directly from the determination of our individuality; how everything ethically outstanding is not inspired by the force of moral law, but accomplished through the direct impulse of an individual idea. Only such a view makes true human freedom possible. If the human spirit does not bear within itself the reason for its actions, but must direct itself according to commandments, it acts under compulsion; it is in this case subject to necessity, almost like a mere creature of nature.

Our philosophy is a philosophy of freedom, therefore, in the highest sense. First it shows theoretically how every force that controls the world externally must fall away before human self-mastery, in the highest sense of the word, can come about. When human beings act in a moral way, in our view this is not merely the fulfillment of duty, but an expression of the wholly free nature of the individual. One acts not through compulsion, but through self-determination. Goethe also had this view in mind when he said,† "Lessing, who was reluctantly aware of many kinds of limitations, causes one of his characters to say, 'No one must *have to.*' A brilliant and happy man said, 'One who wills, *must.*' A third (certainly an educated person) added, *'One who has insight, also wills.'"* Thus, except for our own insight, there is no impulse for our conduct. The free human spirit acts according to its own insight, without the intrusion of any kind of compulsion—*according to self-determined commands.*

The well-known Kant-Schiller controversy revolves around these truths.[†] Kant took the position that duty commands. He believed it degrades moral law to make it dependent upon human subjectivity. In his view, human beings act morally only after banishing all subjective motives and bowing purely to the majesty of duty. Schiller saw this view as a degradation of human nature. Is human nature so evil that its own impulses must be set aside completely before it can be moral? Schiller's and Goethe's worldview can acknowledge only the perspective we have presented. We find the beginning of human action in humanity itself.

Consequently, in history, too—whose subject is humanity—we must not speak of external influences on human conduct, or ideas living in the age, and such. Even less should we speak of a plan that constitutes the basis of history. History is simply the evolution of human actions and views. Goethe said, "In all times, only individuals have worked for knowledge, not the ages themselves. It was the age that put Socrates to death with poison, the age that burned Huss; the ages have always been the same."[†] All conception of plans presumed to be the basis of history contradict the historical method as it arises from the nature of history itself.

The goal of history is to learn what human beings have contributed to the advancement of their group—the goal of this or that personality, and the direction that each individual gave to the age. The entire basis of history should be human nature—understanding the will and the tendencies of human nature. Our epistemology excludes any possibility that we should ascribe a purpose to history—that, for example, the purpose was to raise humanity from a lower stage of perfection to a higher one. Likewise, from our point of view, it is a fallacy to explain historical events as facts of nature according to a succession of cause and effect, as Herder does in *Ideas for a Philosophy of Human History.*

The laws of history are of a far higher kind. In physics, one fact determines another so that the law is above the phenomenon. A historical fact, to the degree that it contains an idea, must be determined by means of ideas. Here, we can speak of cause and effect only when referring exclusively to the external aspects. Who could believe that we keep to the facts by saying that Luther caused the Reformation? History is essentially a science of ideas; ideas constitute its reality. Therefore, devotion to the object is the only correct method. Any step beyond this is not in keeping with history.

Psychology, sociology, and history are the leading forms of cultural science. As we have seen, the basis of their methods is a direct understanding of the reality of ideas. Their subject is the *idea*, the spiritual, just as that of inorganic science is the *natural law*, and that of organics the *type*.

# 20. Optimism and Pessimism

For us, the human being has proven to be the central point of the world-order. As spirit, the human being attains the highest form of existence and, in thought, achieves the most accomplished world-process. Things are real only as the human spirit illuminates them. This is a view according to which the human spirit contains the support, the goal, and the central essence of its existence. It makes the human being self-sufficient, finding within the self the support for everything pertaining to it and, thus, finding happiness within. If happiness comes to us, we have only ourselves to thank. Any power that gives us happiness from without condemns us to a lack of freedom. Before anything can give us happiness, we must first give it that power. In a higher sense, attraction and aversion exist for human beings only to the extent that we experience these as such. Hence, all optimism and all pessimism fall to the ground. The former assumes that everything is good in the world, and that the whole process leads humanity to the greatest contentment. However, this cannot be true unless we must first gain what we long for from the world's objects; in other words, we cannot attain happiness though the world, but only through ourselves.

Pessimism, on the other hand, holds that the world is ordered in such a way that human beings will never be satisfied or happy. Of course, the argument just mentioned applies here, too. The outer world is neither good nor bad in itself; it becomes the one or the other only through us. We must first make ourselves unhappy before pessimism can have any basis. We would have to have an internal longing for misfortune. Nevertheless, the satisfaction of this longing is precisely what provides a basis for our happiness. To be consistent, pessimism would have to assume that people see happiness in misfortune. Then, however, its perspective would again dissolve into nothing. This one consideration alone shows clearly enough the fallacy of pessimism.

# G : Conclusion

## 21. Knowledge and Artistic Creation

Our theory of knowledge has stripped away the mere passivity often associated with cognition and has instead conceived it as an activity of the human spirit. The general assumption is that we receive the substance of knowledge from the outside world; indeed, people believe that knowledge is all the more objective if our mind avoids adding anything of its own. Our discussion has shown that the true content of knowledge is never the external material we perceive, but the *idea* conceived in the mind, which leads us more deeply into the fabric of the world than does any analysis and observation of the external world as mere experience. The idea *is* the content of knowledge. In contrast with the passively received percept, knowledge is thus the product of human mental activity. Thus, we have closely connected the act of cognition with artistic creation, which is also a product of human activity. Nevertheless, we have also brought up the need to clarify the mutual relationship of these two.

The activity of cognition, like that of art, depends on seeing ourselves not as a product of reality but as its producer; that we ascend from created to creator, from chance to necessity. Outer reality always shows us only a creation of working nature, but when we elevate ourselves in spirit to nature's being, we see that it is we who are creating. Every object of reality represents to us one of the endless possibilities hidden in the creative womb of nature. Our mind rises to the vision of the fountainhead that contains all of these possibilities. Science and art are now the objects upon which we impress what this vision offers us. In science, this occurs only in the form of the idea—in the directly mental, or spiritual, medium. In art, it occurs in sensorially or mentally perceptible objects. In science, nature appears purely as idea, "embracing all the separate parts"; in art, an object of the external world appears as a representation of this all-embracing quality. Art impresses the infinite—which science seeks in the finite and endeavors to represent in the idea—upon material taken from the existing world. What appears in science as the *idea* is the *image* in art. The same infinite is the object of both science and of art, but its appearance differs in each; the manner of representation is different. Thus, Goethe criticized the fact that people spoke of the *idea of beauty* as though beauty were not simply a sensory reflection of the idea.[†]

Here we see how a true artist must create from the fountainhead of all existence and how works of art are stamped by necessity, which we see in science as the idea in nature and spirit. Science discovers conformity to law in nature; art does likewise, but it also impresses it onto crude matter. An artistic product is no less a part of nature than is a natural product, except that natural law has been poured into art as it manifests to the human mind. The great works of art that Goethe saw in Italy[†] appeared to him as the direct impressions of what humanity perceived as necessity in nature. Thus to him, art also manifests the hidden laws of nature.[†]

In works of art, everything depends on the degree to which the artist has implanted the idea into the materials. It is not important *what* the artist does, but *how* the artist does it. Science must completely overcome the externally perceived phenomenon so that only its essence (the idea) remains; whereas, in artistic production, the phenomenon must remain, except that the artistic treatment must completely overcome its peculiarities and chance characteristics. The object must be lifted completely above the realm of the chance and moved to that of necessity. No element of chance beauty must remain, which itself has not been impressed by the artist's spirit. *How* must overcome *what.*

The goal of both art and science is to surmount the sensory through the spirit. Science overcomes the sensory by dissolving it wholly into spirit; art impresses spirit into matter. Science sees the idea *through* the sensory; art sees the idea *in* the sensory. Goethe expresses these truths comprehensively in a way that brings our reflections to a close: "I think that science might be called knowledge of the general, or abstract knowledge. Art, on the other hand, would be science applied in an action; science would be reason, and art its mechanism, so that art might also be called practical science. Finally, therefore, science would be the theorem, and art the problem."[†]

# *Notes to the First Edition [1886]*

## [Notes to the Foreword]

* Compare Goethe's natural scientific writings in Kürschner's *Deutscher National-Literatur* [*German National-Literature*], Volume 1, page 115.

* Schröer deals with the manner in which my views fit in with the overall picture of Goethe's worldview in his Foreword to *Goethes Naturwissenschaftliche Schriften* [*Goethe's Natural Scientific Writings*] (Kürschner's *Deutscher National-Literatur*, Vol. 1, pages I-XIV).

[Ed. Note: *Faust von Goethe* (Faust by Goethe). With an introduction and ongoing annotations for volume 2, *Faust II*. Published by K. J. Schröer. First edition. Heilbronn, 1881.]

## [Notes to the Text]

1. Cf. [Karl F. W.] Jessen, *Botanik der Gegenwart und Vorzeit* [*in culturhistorischer Entwicklung*], [Botany of the present and past in cultural-historical development]. [Leipzig, 1864], p. 459.

2. Ibid., p. 343.

3. Ibid., p. 332.

4. Johannes Volkelt, *Immanuel Kants Erkenntnistheorie* [nach ihren Grundprincipien analysirt]. Leipzig, 1879.

5. Johannes Volkelt, *Erfahrung und Denken. Kritische Grundlegung der Erkenntnistheorie.* Hamburg and Leipzig, 1886.

6. *Kants Erkenntnistheorie*, p. 168 f.

7. Cf. Volkelt, *Erfahrung und Denken*, p. 4.

8. Cf. Goethe, *Dichtung und Wahrheit.* [Part 3, Book II] XXII. 24 f.

9. J. H. von Kirchmann says, indeed, in his *Lehre vom Wissen* [als Einleitung in das Studium philosophischer Werke] [Leipzig, 1878, third edition] that cognition is the flowing of the external world into our consciousness.

[Ed. Note: "The manner in which the content or essence of the being flows over into the knowing in the perception and remains the same in both is withdrawn from self-perception and absolutely not conceivable, because the soul cannot grasp or imagine this content or essence itself without a knowledge-form." *Die Lehre vom Wissen als Einleitung in das Studium philosophischer Werke* (The doctrine of knowing as introduction in the study of philosophical works), third edited edition, Leipzig, 1878.]

10. Conceived as a spiritual capacity of the human being.

11. [Goethe's essay, "The Experiment as Mediator between Subject and Object"]. It is interesting that Goethe wrote a second paper in which he pursued further the thoughts of that one regarding the experiment. We can reconstruct the paper from Schiller's letter of January 19, 1798. Goethe there divided the methods of science into general empiricism, which limits itself to the external phenomena, that which is given to the senses; rationalism, which constructs systems of thought on the basis of insufficient observation, and which, therefore, instead of grouping facts according to their essential nature, first cleverly devises the interconnections artificially and then out of this connection introduces something fantastic into the factual world; and, finally, rational empiricism, which does not limit itself to general experience, but creates conditions under which experience discloses its essential nature.

[Ed. Note: In the Weimar edition of Goethe's Complete Works (second part of Volume 11, 1893) it says: "What we have to show for our work would be the following: (1) *The empirical phenomena* that every human being perceives in nature and that afterward will be elevated through experimentation to (2) *scientific phenomena*, because we present it with more or less fortunate results in other circumstances and conditions than we knew it at first. (3) The pure phenomena stands in the end as a result of all experiences and tests. It can never be isolated, but rather shows itself always as the consequence of the manifestations. In order to present it, the human mind determines empirical tottering or instability; eliminates the accidental; separates out the impure; further develops what is confusing and, yes, discovers the unknown."]

12. Haeckel, *Die Naturanschauung von Darwin, Goethe und Lamarck.* [The Conception of Nature of Darwin, Goethe, and Lamarck] [Jena], 1882, p. 53.

# *Annotations to the Edition of 1924*

Page 8: "Educated nonspecialists have the vague feeling that such writings contain nothing of intellectual worth...": The mood underlying this judgment about the character of philosophical writing and the interest that it evokes arises from the mindset characterizing scientific endeavors around the middle of the eighties of the last century. Since that time events have arisen in the light of which this judgment seems no longer justified. One need think only of the dazzling illumination that broad areas of life have received from Nietzsche's thought and perceptivity. And in the struggle that has been in process and still continues between the materialistically minded monists and the defenders of a spiritual worldview there lives both the aspiration of philosophic thought to a life-filled content as well as the widespread general interest in the questions about the riddles of existence. Ways of thought derived from a material worldview, such as those of Einstein, have become the topic of almost universal conversations and literary publications. And yet the motives that then gave rise to that judgment are still active today. Such judgments today would require a different formulation. Now that it reappears, as an almost ancient point of view, it may be appropriate to say to what extent it is still valid.

Goethe's worldview, whose theory of knowledge it has been the purpose of the present book to describe, arises from the inner experience of the *whole* human being. In comparison with this inner experience, the examination of the world through thought is only one aspect. Out of the fullness of human existence, thought-forms rise, as it were, to the surface of the soul's life. A part of these thought-images comprise an answer to the question: What is human cognition? And the form of this answer allows one to see that human existence only reaches its potential when it is engaged in the activity of cognition. A soul-life apart from cognition would be like a human organism without a head: that is, it simply would not be at all. Within the inner life of the soul a content arises that craves external perception as the hungering organism craves food; and in the outer world there is a perceptual content that does not bear its essential being in itself, but shows it only when it is united with soul-content through the process of cognition. Thus the process of cognition becomes a link in the formation of universal reality. In the act of cognizing, one participates in the creation of this universal reality. And if a plant's root is unthinkable apart from the fulfillment of its potentialities in the fruit, so both the individual and the world itself are unable to reach fulfillment without cognition. In the act of cognition, one does not create something only for oneself, but one works together with the world toward the revelation of real being. What is in the human being is the appearance of the Idea; what is in the perceptible world is the appearance of the sensible; only the inter-working of the two in cognition constitutes reality.

Viewed thus, a theory of knowledge becomes a part of life. And it must be viewed thus if it is to be united with the expanses of life in Goethe's soul-experience. But even Nietzsche's thinking and perception do not connect themselves with such breadths of life. Still less is this true of such philosophically oriented conceptions of the world and of life as have appeared since the writing of what has been designated as the "Point of Departure" in the present work. All these presuppose that reality exists somewhere outside of cognition, and that a human representation reproducing this reality should come about in cognition—or cannot come about. That this reality cannot be found by means of cognition because it is first created as reality *in* cognition—this is almost nowhere realized. Those who think philosophically look for life and being outside of knowledge; Goethe stands within creative life and being while he engages in the activity of cognition. For this reason the more recent attempts at world-conceptions take their stand outside of Goethe's creation of ideas. This theory of knowledge wishes to stand within that, because in this way philosophy gains the life-content and the human relevance that are its vital needs.

Page 8: "The task of science is not to raise questions...": Questions regarding knowledge arise in the perception of the external world by the human soul-organization. In the soul's impulse to question lies the power to come close to the perception in such a way that this, together with the activity of the soul, brings to manifestation the reality of what is perceived.

Page 16: "Our initial activity is the sensory comprehension of reality... pure experience.": It is evident from the whole attitude of this theory of knowledge that the main point of its explanations is to gain an answer to the question: "What is knowledge?" In order to reach this goal we focus our attention on the world of sense perception on the one hand, and on that of penetration through thought on the other; and it is pointed out that the true reality of sense existence reveals itself through the penetration of both. In this way the question "What is cognition?" is in principle answered. This answer is not altered if the question is extended to the perception of the spiritual. Therefore, what is said in this book about the essential nature of knowledge holds good also for knowledge of the spiritual worlds, with which my later writings are concerned. The sensory world in its manifestation to human perception is not reality. It achieves its reality in connection with what reveals itself in the human being in the form of thought concerning the sensory world. Thoughts belong to the reality of what is sensibly perceived; though, what is present in sense existence as thought manifests itself not externally in this existence, but inwardly in the human being. But thought and sense perception are *one* in their true being. When one approaches the world in sense perception, one separates thought from reality; but here reality merely manifests itself in another place: within the soul. The separation between percept and thought has no significance for the objective world; it occurs only because one places oneself in the midst of existence. Thereby it appears as if thought and percept were a duality. It is no different for spiritual *perception*. When this occurs by reason of soul processes that I have described in my recent book *Knowledge of the Higher World and Its Attainment*, this then again forms one aspect of (spiritual) existence; and the corresponding *thoughts* of the spiritual form the other aspect. A difference occurs only to the extent that sense perception attains reality through thinking by going, as it were, in an upward direction to the beginning of the spiritual; whereas spiritual *perception* is experienced in its true being going from this starting-point in a downward direction. The fact that the experience of sense perception occurs through the senses *formed by nature*, and that of the perception of the spiritual through spiritual organs of perception first *developed by the soul*, does not constitute a distinction in principle.

In truth, the idea of cognition I developed in this writing is not abandoned in my more recent publications, but is only applied to experience of the spiritual.

[Ed. Note: "In reference to my recent book": (CW 10) was originally published as essays in the magazine *Luzifer-Gnosis*, numbers 13-28, Berlin, from June 1905 - September 1905. First book edition, Berlin, 1909. Published as *How to Know Higher Worlds*, SteinerBooks, 1994.]

Page 17: "In reference to the essay: 'Nature'": In my writings for the Goethe Society, I tried to show that the way this essay originated was that at the time of its writing Tobler had some communication with Goethe in Weimar, and after conversations with him wrote down ideas that lived in Goethe and were acknowledged by him. This essay then appeared in the *Tiefurter Journal*, which was at that time circulated only in manuscript form. Now in Goethe's writings one finds an essay written by him much later concerning the earlier publication. Goethe there expressly states that he did not remember whether the essay was by him, but that it contained ideas that at the time of its appearance were his own. In my discussion through the writings of the Goethe Society, I tried to show that these ideas, as they had evolved, have flowed into Goethe's whole conception of nature. Since then, published discussions attribute complete authorship of the essay "Nature" to Tobler. I do not wish to enter the controversy over this question. Even if complete originality is maintained for Tobler, the fact remains that these ideas lived in Goethe at the beginning of the 1780s, and, indeed, in such a way, that also by his own statement, they proved to be the beginning of his comprehensive conception of nature. Personally I have no reason to abandon my opinion regarding this matter, that the ideas originated with Goethe. But, even if they did not, they lived as a presence in his spirit that has become immeasurably fruitful. To one who is considering Goethe's world-conception, they are significant, not in themselves, but in relationship to what has grown out of them.

[Ed. Note: "In reference to the essay: 'Nature'": See also Rudolf Steiner's essay: " Zu dem 'Fragment' über die Nature" (To the fragment on nature), in the *Schriften der Goethe-Gesellschaft*, Volume 7, 1892. It is now to be found in *Methodische Grundlagen der Anthroposophie. Gesammelte Aufsätze zur Philosophie, Naturwissenschaft, Ästhetik und Seelenkunde 1884-1901* (Methodical foundations of Anthroposophy: collected essays on philosophy, natural science, aesthetics and psychology 1884-1901) (GA 30).

"Tobler": Georg Christoph Tobler (1757-1812), Swiss theologist and philologist (of ancient literature and languages). He met Goethe in Genf in the autumn of 1780 during Goethe's second trip to Switzerland. The following summer Goethe visited him in Weimar.

"*Tierfurter Journal*": Or also *Journal von Tierfurt* (Journal of Tierfurt). It was named after the summer residence of Anna Amelia (1739-1807), Duchess of Sachsen-Weimar-Eisenach. She was the founder of the journal. It came out approximately every three weeks in eleven handwritten copies. It existed until 1784.

"an essay written by him much later": "Erläuterungen zu dem aphoristischen Aufsatz 'Die Natur'" (Explanations for the aphoristic essay "Nature") From Goethe to Chancellor von Müller, Weimar, dated May 24, 1828. In the second part of volume 11 of the Weimar edition of Goethe's works: "I cannot factually remember having written these examinations, but they do agree with what I had thought at that time."]

Page 27: "appearance to the senses...": In this discussion there is already an allusion to the perception of the spiritual, which is treated in my more recent writings in the sense indicated in the above note to page 16.

Page 27: "The situation would be entirely different...": In this discussion the perception of the spiritual is not contradicted, but what is pointed out is that regarding sensory perception it is not possible to reach its real being by forcing a way, so to speak, through the sense-perceptible and pressing forward to the real being behind this sense perception, but only by turning back to what reveals itself in the human being in the element of thought.

Page 78: "No other method of research makes this distinction as consistently as did Goethe.": It will be found that I have expressed myself in various ways in my writings regarding mysticism and the mystical. One can see from the context in each instance that there is no contradiction in these various ways, as some people have fantasized. One may form a general conception of the mystical. According to this, it embraces what may be learned of the world through the soul's inner experience. One cannot argue with this concept for the time being, because there is such an experience. Moreover, it reveals something, not only about our inner being, but also about the world. We need to have eyes in which processes occur in order to experience something about the realm of colors. However, one thus learns something, not only about the eye, but also about the world. One must possess an inner soul-organ in order to experience certain things of the world.

But one must bring full conceptual clarity into one's experience of the mystical organ before knowledge can come about. There are those, however, who want to flee into their inner being in order to escape from conceptual clarity. Their "mysticism" would lead knowledge away from the light of ideas into the darkness of the world of feeling—the world of feeling not illuminated by ideas. Throughout my writings, I have expressed myself against such mysticism.

However, every page in my books supports the mysticism that maintains the clarity of ideas in thinking and makes the mystic sense a perceptual organ of the soul that functions in the same region of the human being where otherwise obscure feelings dominate. With respect to the spiritual, this sense is entirely the equivalent of an eye or ear in relation to the physical.

Page 91: "Philosophy of freedom": The ideas of this philosophy were later further developed in my *Philosophy of Spiritual Activity* (1894).

[Ed. Note: German title *Die Philosophie der Freiheit* (1894). *Intuitive Thinking as a Spiritual Path: A Philosophy of Freedom*, Anthroposophic Press, 1995.]

Page 93: "Psychology, sociology, and history are the leading forms of cultural science": After having elaborated the various aspects of what I call

"Anthroposophy," I would have to insert Anthroposophy here—if I were writing the present book today. Forty years ago, when I was writing it, I visualized psychology—though not in the usual sense of the term—as something that includes the perception of the entire world of spirit (pneumatology). But it must not be concluded from this that I then intended to exclude this world of spirit from human knowledge.

[Ed note: See, for example, Rudolf Steiner, *A Psychology of Body, Soul, and Spirit: Anthroposophy, Psychosophy, Pneumatosophy*, Anthroposophic Press, 1999.]

Page 100: [Annotation to footnote 11 in the first edition] Footnote 11 should now be supplemented by the statement that the essay that I here hypothetically assumed was later actually found in the Goethe and Schiller Museum and included in the Weimar edition of Goethe.

# REFERENCE NOTES

**Page 1, "Otto Liebmann"**
Otto Liebmann (1840-1912) was a German philosopher and a forerunner of neo-Kantian thought. In his best known book *Kant und die Epigonen* (Stuttgart 1865), he deals with philosophy after Kant, discussing Fichte, Schelling, Hegel, Fries, Herbart, and Schopenhauer. Having credited Kant's philosophy (though criticizing it on the vital point of accepting a thing-in-itself), he focuses on what he sees as the shortcomings in the approaches of Kant's successors. He frequently ends a section with the statement that one should return to Kant.

*Zur Analysis der Wirklichkeit.* A discussion of the foundational problems of philosophy. In the third, improved and expanded edition, Strassburg, 1900, on page 28 it says: "It is inconsistent to want to maintain that the imagined object is *not* outside of subjective thinking, precisely because as a thinking subject, one cannot come out of one's own subjective thinking; it is never possible to rise above one's own consciousness and be free of oneself, so as to be able to state what does exist or does not exist in one's subjectivity." See also Otto Liebmann's *Gedanken und Thatsachen: Philosophische Abhandlungen, Aphorismen und Studien* [Thoughts and facts: philosophical treatments, aphorisms, and studies], Strassburg, 1882 (later new editions in several volumes). See also *Die Klimax der Theorieen: eine Untersuchung aus dem Bereich der allgemeinen Wissenschaftslehre* [The high point of the theories: an examination out of the sphere of general scientific doctrine], Strassburg, 1884.

For Liebmann and Volkelt, compare the chapter, "Echoes of the Kantian Mode of Conception," in Rudolf Steiner's *The Riddles of Philosophy* (CW 18), Anthroposophic Press, 1973.

**Page 1, "Johannes Volkelt"**
"*Kant's Theory of Knowledge,*" Johannes Volkelt, *Immanuel Kants Erkenntnistheorie*, Hamburg, 1879.

"*Experience and Thinking,*" Johannes Volkelt, *Erfahrung and Denken*, Hamburg, 1886.

**Page 2, "Eduard von Hartmann"**
Karl Robert Eduard von Hartmann (1842-1906) was a German whose reputation as a philosopher was established by his first book, *The Philosophy of the Unconscious* (1869). The book's success was owed largely to the originality of its title, the diversity of its contents (von Hartmann professing to obtain his speculative results by the methods of inductive science and making plentiful use

of concrete illustrations), the fashionableness of its pessimism, and the vigor and lucidity of its style. The concept of the unconscious, by which von Hartmann describes his ultimate metaphysical principle, is not really as paradoxical as it sounds, being merely a new and mysterious designation for the Absolute of German metaphysicians.

Compare *Beiträge zur Rudolf Steiner Gesamtausgabe* [Contributions to Rudolf Steiner's complete works], Number 85/86, 1984: "Zur Philosophie der Freiheit: Kommentare und Randbemerkungen von Eduard von Hartmann." [On the Philosophy of Freedom: commentary and margin notes by Eduard von Hartmann]. Also contained in this issue is "Rudolf Steiner und [and] Eduard von Hartmann" by Andreas Neider.

**Page 3, "essay on atomism, which was never published"**
The manuscript of this essay, which was long considered lost, was found upon the reorganization of Friedrich Theodore Vischer's estate when it was transferred to the library at Tübingen University, Tübingen, Germany. It was then published by C. S. Picht in the weekly periodical, *Das Goetheanum* [The Goetheanum], Year 18, Number 22 from May 28, 1939 and Number 23 from June 4, 1939. The 21-year-old Rudolf Steiner sent the essay, with the title "Einzig mögliche Kritik der atomistischen Begriffe" [Only possible critique of the concepts of atomism], along with an accompanying letter to Vischer. This essay and the accompanying letter are published in *Beiträge zur Rudolf Steiner Gesamtausgabe* [Contributions to Rudolf Steiner's complete works], Number 63, 1978.

**Page 3, "During the 1880s, Karl Julius Schröer"**
Karl Julius Schröer (1825-1900) was an extraordinary educator, philologist, and Goethe scholar. In 1867, Schröer was professor of the History of German Literature at the technical college in Vienna, where Steiner met him. He became the "fatherly friend" and sponsor of Steiner during the 1880s.

Compare Rudolf Steiner's *Autobiography* (CW 28), Chapter 17. This work was edited and annotated by Rudolf Steiner and included a foreword by Professor K. J. Schröer. It was published by Joseph Kürschner with the title *Goethes Naturwissenschaftliche Schriften* (Goethe's natural scientific writings) in *Deutscher National-Literatur* [German national literature] in five volumes: Volume 1: *Bildung und Umbildungen organischer Naturen. Zur Morphologie* (1883) [Forming and transformation of organic nature. On metamorphosis.]; Volume 2: *Zur Naturwissenschaft im Allgemeinen. Mineralogie und Geologie. Meteorolgie* (1887) [On general natural science. Mineralogy and geology. Meteorology]; Volume 3: *Beiträge zur Optik. Zur Farbenlehre. Enthüllung der Theorie Newtons* (1890) [Contributions to optics. On the theory of color. Unveiling Newton's theory]; Volume 4: *Zur Farbenlehre. Materialien zur Geschichte der Farbenlehre* (1897) [Materials for the theory of color]; and Volume 5: *Materialien zur Geschicte der Farbenlehre (Schluß). Entoptische Farben. Paralipomena zur Chromatk. Sprüche in*

*Prosa. Nachträge* (1897) [Materials for the theory of color (last part). Invisible colors. Things left out of chromatics. Sayings in prose. Addenda]. Reprinted in Dornach as GA 1a-e, 1975.

**Page 4, "*The Riddles of Philosophy*"**
Published first in two volumes with the title *Welt und Lebensanchauungen im 19. Jahrhundert* [World and philosophy of life in the nineteenth century], Berlin, in 1900 and 1901. Then published in 1914 under the present title of *Die Rätsel der Philosophie in ihrer Geschicte als Umriß dargestellt* [The riddles of philosophy, an outline of its history]. *The Riddles of Philosophy* (CW 18), Anthroposphic Press, 1973.

**Page 5, "in his paper "Anschauende Urteilskraft"**
"Anschauende Urteilskraft" [Power of discernment in seeing]. "... yet when in the moral-ethical element through belief in God, virtue, and immortality we raise ourselves up to a higher region and want to approach the first beings there, it is possible that this is the same case in the intellect, that through looking at an ever-creating nature we make ourselves worthy of spiritual participation in its productions." *Goethes Naturwissenschaflichen Schriften* [Goethe's natural scientific writings], Volume 1 (entire essay).

**Page 9, "The latter calls Hegel a charlatan"**
Schopenhauer said in comment to a sentence by Hegel: "I do not think it is difficult to understand that a person is a shameless charlatan who wants to beguile the simpleton and feels that he has found his people in the German folk of the nineteenth century." From his *Parerga und Paralipomena: Skizze einer Geschichte der Lehre vom Idealen und Realen* [Addenda and omissions: sketch of a history of the doctrine of the ideal and the real]. An appendix in the *Sämtliche Werke*, Volume 8, Stuttgart, 1894. [Complete works], edited by Rudolf Steiner.

**Page 9, "their unlimited admiration for Goethe"**
Hegel's admiration:
See, for example, Hegel's letter to Goethe of February 21, 1821. Goethe published this letter, titled "Neuste aufmunternde Teilnahme" [Most recent encouraging interest], in the supplement to the theory of color (with the date of February 20). *Goethes Naturwissenschaftlichen Schriften*, Volume 5, with annotations by Rudolf Steiner. Compare also the chapter titled "Goethe and Hegel" in Rudolf Steiner's *Goethe's Worldview* (CW 6).

Schopenhauer's admiration:
In 1813-14 Schopenhauer enjoyed a personal social relationship with Goethe and was introduced to the theory of color. Based on this he wrote his own treatment, "Über das Sehen und die Farben" [About vision and colors], and sent it to Goethe at the beginning of June 1815. See *Goethe-Jahrbuch IX* [Book of essays, reports, and so forth, put out usually annually by a library or institution], Frankfurt,

1888. See also Arthur Schopenhauer's *Der Brief wechsel mit Goethe und andere Documente zur Farbenlehre* [Correspondence with Goethe and other documents for the theory of color], published by Ludger Lütkehaus, Zurich, 1992.

**Page 9-10, "Haeckel ... sees the anticipation of his own view in that of Goethe"**
Ernst Haeckel (1834-1919) in his *Die Naturanschauung von Darwin, Goethe und Lamarck* [The view of nature of Darwin, Goethe, and Lamarck]. A lecture in Eisenach on September 18, 1882. Published in Jena in 1882.

**Page 10, "K. F. W. Jessen ... supported by many pretentious arguments"**
Literally: "...theory supported by many pretexts...." Karl F. W Jessen, *Botanik der Gegenwart und der Vorzeit in culture-historischer Entwickelung. Ein Beitrag zur Geschichte der abendländischen Völker* [Modern and ancient Botany in the history of cultural development], Leipzig, 1864.

**Page 10, "The poet is the only true human being."**
In a letter from Friedrich Schiller to Goethe on January 7, 1795: "This much is certain: that the poet is the only true human being, and the best philosopher is only a caricature in comparison." *Briefwechsel zwischen Schiller und Goethe in den Jahren 1794 bis 1805* [Correspondence between Schiller and Goethe from 1974-1805], Part 1, from 1794 and 1795. Stuttgart and Tübingen, 1828.

**Page 13, "In his letters on the aesthetic education of humankind"**
Friedrich Schiller, titled in German: *Über die aesthetische Erziehung des Menschen, in einer Reihe von Briefen* [About the aesthetic education of the human being] in a cycle of letters, 1795.

His essay on naïve and sentimental poetry is titled in German: "Über naïve und sentimentalische Dichtung," 1795/96.

**Page 14, "that we must return to Kant"**
Otto Liebmann, *Kant, und die Epigonen. Eine Kritische Abhandlung* [Kant, and the epigons/successors. A critical treatment], Stuttgart, 1865. The final sentence of almost every chapter is: "...we must return to Kant."

**Page 15, "Theory, in and of itself, is useless"**
*Goethes Nuturwissenschaftliche Schriften*, [Goethe's natural scientific writings] Volume 5: Sprüche in Prosa [Sayings in prose].

**Page 17, "We are surrounded and embraced by her..."**
Literally: "Nature! We are surrounded and embraced by her—unable to leave her, unable to enter more deeply into her. Unasked and unwarned, she takes us into the cycle of her dance and carries us away with her, until we are exhausted and fall out of her arms." *Goethes Naturwisseschaftlichen Schriften*, Volume 2: *Zur*

*Naturwissenschaft im Allgemeinen* [On natural science in general], first paragraph of the text with the title, "Die Natur. Aphoristisch" [Nature. Aphoristic.]

**Page 21, "such as rain beginning outside"**
Literally: "among others, also one with the content that it is beginning to rain outside." Johannes Volkelt, *Emmanuel Kant's Erkenntnisstheorie nach ihren Grundprincipien analysirt. Ein Beitrag zur Grundlegung der Erkenntnisstheorie* [Analysis of Emmanuel Kant's theory of knowledge according to its foundational principles. A contribution to laying the foundation of the theory of knowledge.], Leipzig, 1879.

**Page 22, "*Gehirn und Bewußtsein*"**
Richard Wahle (1857-1935), Austrian Professor of Philosophy and Pedagogy in Czernowitz, and later in Vienna. *Gehirn und Bewußtsein. Physiologisch-psychologische Studie* [Brain and consciousness. Physiological-pschological study], Vienna, 1884. Also: "Nothing else shows itself other than objects standing beside one another.... Their actual standing beside one another is because each object exists of itself in its place, separately, without having anything to do with the others. The trees of the forest do not enter into a relationship with each other. They are not encompassed by any kind of unity; they are simply beside one another. Thus, also the thoughts, which are the same as objects, are beside one another."

**Page 23, "a bias that has persisted since the time of Kant"**
*The Critique of Pure Reason.* A transcendental basic doctrine, first part, general remarks on the transcendental aesthetics: "We have thus wanted to say that all of our vision is only the imagination of the appearance. The thing that we look at is not the way we see it, nor are its relationships what they appear to us. If we were to remove our self, our individual being, or even just the subjective nature of the senses, all that makes up relationships in time and space—yes, even time and space—would disappear, and would no longer exist of themselves, but could exist only in us." Quote from the edition by Karl Vorländer, Halle on the Saale, 1899.

**Page 24, "Volkelt asserts..."**
Johannes Volkelt, *Erfahrung und Denken. Kritische Grundlegung der Erkenntnistheorie* [Experience and thinking. Critical foundation-laying of the theory of knowledge], Volume 1, Hamburg and Leipzig, 1886.

**Page 31, "we must find the means within nature itself"**
Johann Wolfgang Goethe, *Poetry and Truth* [actual intended meaning of the title: *Dichtung und Wahrheit*: Fiction and truth]. Literal quote about Paul Thiry d'Holbach's *Système de la nature*: "He may have known just as little about nature as we, for he piles up several general concepts and then abandons them immediately in order to change what is higher than nature, or what appears as higher

nature in nature into material, heavy, indeed animated, but directionless and formless nature. And he believed thereby to have attained quite a lot." Johann Wolfgang Goethe, *Sämtliche Werke nach Epochen seines Schaffens* [Collected works arranged according to categories], Munich Edition, Volume 16, Munich, 1985.

**Page 46, "If the eye were not sun-like"**
Goethe, "Zahme Xenien" [Tame Xenia], III. A slight variation in *Goethes Naturwissenschaftliche Schriften* [Goethe's natural scientific writings], Volume 3: *Entwurf einer Farbenlehre. Didaktischer Teil.* [Outline of a theory of color. Didactic part.] Introduction: "...How could we see the light?"

**Page 50, "Kant pointed out the difference between intellect and reason"**
See, for instance, *The Critique of Pure Reason*, the second part; "The Transcendental Dialectic," Introduction 2a: About Reason: "All of our knowledge begins with the senses; goes from there to the intellect; and ends with reason, of which there is nothing higher found in us to process the object of our vision and to bring it into the highest unity of thinking."

**Page 51, "structures that manifest through reason are mere fantasy, or illusions"**
Ibid. See the doctrine for transcendental methods. The discipline of pure reason in looking at hypotheses: "The concepts of reason are, as said, mere ideas and have no reality in any experience. Therefore, they do not describe composed or thought-up realities that are assumed to be possible. They are merely thought in relation to a problem, in order to found, in relation to this newest fiction, a regulative principle of the systematic application of the intellect in the field of experience."

Compare also Rudolf Steiner's *The Riddles of Philosophy* (CW 18), the chapter titled "The Age of Kant and Goethe."

**Page 56, "The idea is eternal and unique"**
*Goethes Naturwissenschaftliche Schriften* [Goethe's natural scientific writings], Volume 5: *Sprüche in Prosa* [Sayings in prose].

**Page 68, "They call this method *rational empiricism*"**
After Goethe sent his essay, "Der Versuch als Vermittler von Object und Subject," [The experiment as mediator between object and subject] (contained in *Goethes Naturwissenschaftliche Schriften*, [Goethe's natural scientific writings], Volume 2: *Zur Wissenschaft im Allgemeinen* [On science in general]), on January 10, 1798, Schiller answered on January 12, 1798: Your essay contains an excellent idea and at the same time an account of your experience with nature and touches on the highest concern and requirements of rational empiricism by attempting to apply the rule only to isolated, individual matters." And in a letter on January 19, 1798, after he received from Goethe, on January 13, 1798, a

letter and a further untitled essay on pure phenomena (in the Weimar Goethe Edition, part 2, Volume 11, with the title *Erfahrung und Wissenschaft* [Experience and science]), Schiller wrote: "Only *rational empiricism* can penetrate into *pure phenomena*, which I judge to be one with the objective law of nature." Goethe's answer on January 20, 1798: " I am deeply grateful for your examination of my essay in relation to these categories; I will always bear you in mind with my work." "Briefwechsel zwischen Goethe und Schiller in den Jahren 1794 bis 1805," [Correspondence between Goethe an Schiller from 1794-1805]. Part 4 from the year 1798, Stuttgart and Tübingen, 1829.

Compare also Goethe's *Sämtliche Werke nach Epochen seines Schaffens* [Collected works arranged according to categories], Munich edition, Volume 8.2, Munich, 1990: "Kommentar zum 'Briefwechsel'" [Commentary on the correspondence], and in Volume 6.2, Munich 1988, the text of "Das reine Phanomen" [Pure phenomena] and later in the same volume, "Kommentar" [Commentary].

**Page 71, "even sought to give a philosophic basis for this view"**
Kant, *Critique of Judgment*, Hackett, 1987. See in the second part: "Critique of Theological Judgment," 2: On the Characteristic of Human Reason: "Our reason is a treasury of concepts, that is, a discursive reason.... Our reason has, namely, the characteristic that in its knowledge, for instance of the origin of an object, it must proceed from the *analytical-general* to the specific...."

**Page 71, "He was never concerned with the use of something..."**
Compare Eckermann's *Gespräche mit Goethe* [Conversations with Goethe], on February 21, 1831: "Such doctrines on usefulness say that the ox has horns in order to defend itself. Yet I ask: why don't sheep have them? And when they do, why are they wound around their ears, so they are of no use? ... The question of the purpose, the question '*why?*' is absolutely not scientific. Somewhat further on, one comes to the question '*How?*' Then when I ask myself *how* the ox has horns, that leads me to the observation and contemplation of its organization and teaches me at the same time, why the lion has no horns nor can have them." Johann Wolfgang Goethe, *Sämtliche Werke nach Epochen seines Schaffens* [Collected works arranged according to categories], Volume 19, Munich, 1986.

**Page 71, "Goethe was attracted especially to Spinoza"**
Compare *Goethes Nuturwissenschaftliche Schriften* [Goethe's natural scientific writings], Volume 1: "Introductions."

**Page 73, "Haeckel's intention is clear in his demand..."**
Literally: "We may well demand that all subjects of instruction be handled with the genetic method, then the foundational idea of the doctrine of evolution will assert itself everywhere." Ernst Haeckel, "Die Naturanschauung von Darwin, Goethe und Lamarck" [The view of nature of Darwin, Goethe, and Lamarck]. A lecture given at the first public meeting in Eisenach, September 18, 1882, of

the fifty-fifth Versammlung Deutscher Naturforscher und Ärtzte [Assembly of German natural scientists and physicians], Jena, 1882.

**Page 73, "If the mechanics of the soul"**
Ernst Haeckel, "Freie Wissenschaft und freie Lehre. Eine Entgegnung auf Rudolf Virchow's Münchner Rede über 'Die Freiheit der Wissenschaft im modernen Staat'" [Free science and free teaching. A reply to Rudolf Virchow's lecture on the freedom of science in the modern state], Stuttgart, 1878. In his lecture, Virchow objected to the teaching of the doctrine of evolution in schools because it was an unproved hypothesis.

**Page 74, "What Agassiz called 'an embodied creative idea of God.'"**
Louis Agassiz (1807-1873) was a Swiss paleontologist, geologist, and biologist who taught many years in North America. See his work: *Contributions to the Natural History of the United States of America*, Volume 1, Part 1: "Essay on Classification," Boston, 1857. Compare Haeckel's exposition on Agassiz in his *Natürliche Schöpfungsgeschichte* [Natural history of creation]. Popular scientific lectures on the doctrine of evolution in general, and that of Darwin, Goethe, and Lamarck specifically, Berlin, 1874 (fifth edition). Quote found there: "Every individual species of animal, as Agassiz put it, is an embodied creation-thought of God."

**Page 75, "Friedrich Theodor Vischer"**
*Altes und Neues* [Old and new], three notebooks in one volume. Stuttgart, 1881/82. Third Notebook: "Carl Gustav Reuschle, Philosophie und Naturwissenschaft" [Carl Gustav Reuschle, philosophy and science]: "Thus there is a second world above the physical, a moral type or genus above the physiological. For both, what has come into being in time, remains timeless. We need a correction of the concept of time, as I already said about the critical processes in my the sixth notebook, where I spoke of the connection of inner usefulness or purposefulness and the opposite, of outer purposefulness."

**Page 79, "The English philosopher Reid describes intuition"**
Thomas Reid, Scottish philosopher, founder of the Scottish School and the philosophy of common sense. *An Inquiry into the Human Mind on the Principles of Common Sense*, Charlestown, 1813. In chapter 2: " I beg leave to make use of the word *suggestion* because I know not one more proper to express a power of the mind, which seems entirely to have escaped the notice of philosophers, and to which we owe many of our simple notions that are neither impressions or ideas, as well as many original principles of belief." Quoted from the edition published in Chicago and London, 1970.

**Page 79, "Jacobi thought that our feeling of God..."**
"The original revelation of God to human beings is not a revelation in word or image, but the rising up of an inner feeling." Friedrich Heinrich Jacobi's *Werke*,

in 6 volumes, Leipzig, 1812-1825. Volume 3, 1816. Compare also in the same volume: "Von göttlichen Dingen" [About divine things]: "Such a direct, positive truth reveals itself to us in and with the feeling of a drive beyond all perceptible, changeable, accidental interests. This drive announces itself irresistibly as the fundamental drive of human nature."

**Page 79, "Our power of judgment must perceive..."**
See Goethe's essays, "Bedeutende Fördernis durch ein einziges geistreiches Wort" [Significant support through a single brilliant word], in *Goethes Naturwissenschaftlichen Schriften* [Goethe's natural scientific writings], Volume 2, and in the same volume, see "Anschauende Urteilskraft" [Power of intuitive judgment]. Also compare Kant in his *Critique of Judgment*: "Now we can also imagine an intellect that, while it is not discursive like ours but is intuitive, goes from the synthesis in general (the seeing of the whole) to the particular, the specific; that is, from the whole to the parts...."

**Page 86, "Fichte assigned an existence to human individuals..."**
See, for instance, Johann Gottlieb Fichte, *Foundations of the Entire Science of Knowledge, in Fichte: Science of Knowledge [Wissenschaftslehre]*, New York: Appleton-Century-Crofts, 1970; 2nd ed., Cambridge: Cambridge University Press, 1982. There he says: "The 'I' sets or establishes itself, and exists through the mere act of establishing; and vice versa, the 'I' *is*, and it establishes its existence by the mere act of existing. It is at the same time the one acting and the result of the acting; it is the active one and the result that is brought into being through the action. Action and accomplished deed are one and the same, and therefore, the 'I am' is the expression of a deed-action, an action that is also the accomplished deed. This is the only possibility in the whole of scientific doctrine.... That whose existence (being) exists only because it establishes itself as existing is the 'I' as absolute subject. Thus, the way it establishes itself determines its existance; and thus, the manner of its existance establishes it. And the 'I' is absolute and is necessary for the 'I.' What does not exist for itself is not an 'I'." Quoted from Volume 1 of *Johann Gottlieb Fichtes sämtliche Werke*, in 8 volumes, published by I. H. Fichte, Berlin, 1845/46.

**Page 87, "Jacobi is mistaken..."**
Compare F. H. Jacobi, "Über eine Weissagung Lichtenbergs," in Volume 3 of his collected works: "The human being, through his or her own spirit, is incomparable, self-contained, and requires nothing else in order to exist. This spirit belongs to the human being and is what determines who he or she is—this spirit of itself and no other.... Human beings discover themselves to be this, their own being, through a direct feeling of being, a feeling that does not depend on memory of past circumstances, not through knowledge. We know we are this one being and that no one else is this being or can be. We know this because direct *spirit-certainty* is inseparable from the *spirit*, from the selfhood, from the substantiality."

**Page 88, "theory of the soul without soul"**
Friedrich Albert Lange (1825-1875) coined the expression "psychology without soul" in *Geschichte des Materialismus und Kritik seiner Bedeutung in der Gegenwart* [History of materialism and critique of its significance in the present], Iserlohn, 1866. From Volume 2, *Die Naturwissenschaftliche Psychologie* [The natural scientific psychology], 7th edition, Leipzig, 1902: "Yet does psychology not mean doctrine or teaching without soul?" ... Now there we have another fine example of the confusing of the name with the thing! We have a traditional name for a large, but in no way sharply delineated, group of manifestations.... Shall we reject it because the object of science has changed? That would be impractical pedantry. Thus a psychology without soul should be accepted!"

**Page 89, "It is not the intelligent person who rules..."**
*Goethes Naurwissenschaftliche Schriften* [Goethe's natural scientific writings], Volume 5: *Sprüche in Prosa* [sayings in prose].

**Page 89, "The rational world..."**
*Goethes Naurwissenschaftliche Schriften* [Goethe's natural scientific writings], Volume 5: *Sprüche in Prosa* [sayings in prose].

**Page 91, "The world-foundation has poured itself..."**
Compare Goethe's poem "Proemion" [Proemion] in the poetry collection *Gott und Welt* [God and world].

**Page 91, "Kreyenbühl"**
"Die ethische Freiheit bei Kant: eine kritisch-speculative Studie über den wahren Geist der Kant'schen Philosophie" [The ethical freedom in Kant: a critical-speculative study of the true spirit of Kant's philosophy] in *Philosophische Monatshefte*, [Philosophical monthly] XVIII, Heidelberg, 1882.

**Page 91, "Goethe also had this view in mind when he said"**
*Goethes Naurwissenschaftliche Schriften* [Goethe's natural scientific writings], Volume 5: *Sprüche in Prosa* [sayings in prose]. In the original all of his sayings are in italics.

**Page 92, "The well-known Kant-Schiller controversy revolves around these truths"**
See Kant, *The Critique of Practical Reason*, Cambridge University Press, 1997 (4th edition 2003). In the third main piece on the motivating force of practical reason in the first part of the first book: "It is of greatest importance, in all moral judgments, to pay attention with the greatest exactitude to the subjective principle of all maxims. This is important so that all the morality of the actions, in the necessity for the moral aspect, would be established out of duty to and out of respect for the law [of reason], and not out of love and inclination for what the

action is to bring forth. For all human beings and all created beings who possess reason, moral necessity is compulsion; that means, the manner of acting is to be thought of as obligation, and every action based on this as duty, not however as something already loved by us, or that can be loved by us."

See also the well-known passage: 'Duty! You lofty name, that embraces no favor or flattery, but rather demands subjection, yet threatens with nothing that would stimulate disinclination or shocks the mind and soul, in order to move the will. You merely set up a law that finds entrance into the mind and soul on its own. Yet in spite of yourself you gain—even though not always immediate compliance—veneration, before which all inclinations become silent, even though they work against it (the reverence) secretly. What is your worthy origin? Where does one find the root of your noble descent that proudly refuses all relationship with inclinations, and from which root the strict condition is to come for that merit that the human being alone can give himself or herself."

Schiller's argument is to be found, among other places, in his piece "Über Anmut und Würde" [On grace and dignity] in *Sämtliche Werke* [Complete works], Volume 5, Munich, 1962. "Just as convinced as I am—and precisely because I am convinced—that an inclination toward taking part in a free deed means nothing in relation to the pure duty-nature of this deed, so too do I believe that I can conclude from this that the moral perfection of human beings can become evident precisely because of the part their inclination plays in their moral deeds. Human beings are not appointed to do individual moral actions, but to become moral beings. Their instructions are not for [individual] *virtues* but for *the virtue*, and virtue is nothing other than an inclination toward duty. As much as actions out of inclination and actions out of duty stand in opposition to one another in the objective sense, it is not so in the subjective sense. And human being not only *may* but *should* bring duty and inclination into connection with each other. They should obey their reason with joy.... In Kant's philosophy of morality the idea of duty is presented with a hardness from which all the graces shrink back, and which would make a weak intellect seek moral perfection on the path of a dark and monkish aesthetics."

See also his "Xenien" in Volume 1 of the same complete works.

> "Cripple of the conscience
> Gladly I serve the friends, but I do it, unfortunately, out of inclination,
> And so, rankles me often that I am not virtuous.
>
> "Decisum"
> There is no other advice than that you must seek to dislike them,
> And then, with disgust, do what duty tells you."

**Page 92, "In all times, only individuals have worked for knowledge..."**
Friedrich Wilhel Riemer, "Mitteilungen über Goethe" [Communications about Goethe], September 26, 1807. Leipzig, 1921.

Also compare *Goethes Gespräche* [Goethe's conversations], in 10 Volumes. See Volume 2. Published by Woldemar Freiherr von Biedermann. Leipzig, 1889-1896.

**Page 97, "Thus Goethe criticized..."**
"In aesthetics one does not do well to speak of the idea of the beautiful; through this one isolates the beautiful, and it can never be thought by itself, as something isolated."

*Goethes Naurwissenschaftliche Schriften* [Goethe's natural scientific writings], Volume 5: *Sprüche in Prosa* [sayings in prose].

**Page 97, "The great works of art that Goethe saw in Italy"**
"The lofty works of art were produced according to the true and natural laws as the highest work of nature from the human being. Everything arbitrary and imaginary collapses. There is necessity; there is God." In "Rome, September 6, 1787," *Italian Journey*, UK: Collins, 1962; Penguin, 1970.

**Page 97, "art also manifests the hidden laws of nature"**
"The beautiful is a manifestation of secret laws of nature that, without their appearance, would remain eternally hidden." *Goethes Naurwissenschaftliche Schriften* [Goethe's natural scientific writings], Volume 5: *Sprüche in Prosa* [sayings in prose].

**Page 98, "I think that science might be called knowledge..."**
*Goethes Naurwissenschaftliche Schriften* [Goethe's natural scientific writings], Volume 5: *Sprüche in Prosa* [sayings in prose].

# RUDOLF STEINER'S COLLECTED WORKS

The German Edition of Rudolf Steiner's Collected Works (the Gesamtausgabe [GA] published by Rudolf Steiner Verlag, Dornach, Switzerland) presently runs to over 354 titles, organized either by type of work (written or spoken), chronology, audience (public or other), or subject (education, art, etc.). For ease of comparison, the Collected Works in English [CW] follows the German organization exactly. A complete listing of the CWs follows with literal translations of the German titles. Other than in the case of the books published in his lifetime, titles were rarely given by Rudolf Steiner himself, and were often provided by the editors of the German editions. The titles in English are not necessarily the same as the German; and, indeed, over the past seventy-five years have frequently been different, with the same book sometimes appearing under different titles.

For ease of identification and to avoid confusion, we suggest that readers looking for a title should do so by CW number. Because the work of creating the Collected Works of Rudolf Steiner is an ongoing process, with new titles being published every year, we have not indicated in this listing which books are presently available. To find out what titles in the Collected Works are currently in print, please check our website at www.steinerbooks.org, or write to SteinerBooks 610 Main Street, Great Barrington, MA 01230:

**Written Work**

| | |
|---|---|
| CW 1 | Goethe: Natural-Scientific Writings, Introduction, with Footnotes and Explanations in the text by Rudolf Steiner |
| CW 2 | Outlines of an Epistemology of the Goethean World View, with Special Consideration of Schiller |
| CW 3 | Truth and Science |
| CW 4 | The Philosophy of Freedom |
| CW 4a | Documents to "The Philosophy of Freedom" |
| CW 5 | Friedrich Nietzsche, A Fighter against His Own Time |
| CW 6 | Goethe's Worldview |
| CW 6a | Now in CW 30 |
| CW 7 | Mysticism at the Dawn of Modern Spiritual Life and Its Relationship with Modern Worldviews |
| CW 8 | Christianity as Mystical Fact and the Mysteries of Antiquity |
| CW 9 | Theosophy: An Introduction into Supersensible World Knowledge and Human Purpose |
| CW 10 | How Does One Attain Knowledge of Higher Worlds? |
| CW 11 | From the Akasha-Chronicle |
| CW 12 | Levels of Higher Knowledge |

CW 43 Stage Adaptations
CW 44 On the Four Mystery Dramas. Sketches, Fragments and Paralipomena on the Four Mystery Dramas
CW 45 Anthroposophy: A Fragment from the Year 1910

**Public Lectures**

CW 51 On Philosophy, History and Literature
CW 52 Spiritual Teachings Concerning the Soul and Observation of the World
CW 53 The Origin and Goal of the Human Being
CW 54 The Riddles of the World and Anthroposophy
CW 55 Knowledge of the Supersensible in Our Times and Its Meaning for Life Today
CW 56 Knowledge of the Soul and of the Spirit
CW 57 Where and How Does One Find the Spirit?
CW 58 The Metamorphoses of the Soul Life. Paths of Soul Experiences: Part One
CW 59 The Metamorphoses of the Soul Life. Paths of Soul Experiences: Part Two
CW 60 The Answers of Spiritual Science to the Biggest Questions of Existence
CW 61 Human History in the Light of Spiritual Research
CW 62 Results of Spiritual Research
CW 63 Spiritual Science as a Treasure for Life
CW 64 Out of Destiny-Burdened Times
CW 65 Out of Central European Spiritual Life
CW 66 Spirit and Matter, Life and Death
CW 67 The Eternal in the Human Soul. Immortality and Freedom
CW 68 Public lectures in various cities, 1906-1918
CW 69 Public lectures in various cities, 1906-1918
CW 70 Public lectures in various cities, 1906-1918
CW 71 Public lectures in various cities, 1906-1918
CW 72 Freedom – Immortality – Social Life
CW 73 The Supplementing of the Modern Sciences through Anthroposophy
CW 73a Specialized Fields of Knowledge and Anthroposophy
CW 74 The Philosophy of Thomas Aquinas
CW 75 Public lectures in various cities, 1906-1918
CW 76 The Fructifying Effect of Anthroposophy on Specialized Fields
CW 77a The Task of Anthroposophy in Relation to Science and Life: The Darmstadt College Course
CW 77b Art and Anthroposophy. The Goetheanum-Impulse

CW 78 Anthroposophy, Its Roots of Knowledge and Fruits for Life
CW 79 The Reality of the Higher Worlds
CW 80 Public lectures in various cities, 1922
CW 81 Renewal-Impulses for Culture and Science–Berlin College Course
CW 82 So that the Human Being Can Become a Complete Human Being
CW 83 Western and Eastern World-Contrast. Paths to Understanding It through Anthroposophy
CW 84 What Did the Goetheanum Intend and What Should Anthroposophy Do?

**Lectures to the Members of the Anthroposophical Society**

CW 88 Concerning the Astral World and Devachan
CW 89 Consciousness–Life–Form. Fundamental Principles of a Spiritual-Scientific Cosmology
CW 90 Participant Notes from the Lectures during the Years 1903-1905
CW 91 Participant Notes from the Lectures during the Years 1903-1905
CW 92 The Occult Truths of Ancient Myths and Sagas
CW 93 The Temple Legend and the Golden Legend
CW 93a Fundamentals of Esotericism
CW 94 Cosmogony. Popular Occultism. The Gospel of John. The Theosophy in the Gospel of John
CW 95 At the Gates of Theosophy
CW 96 Origin-Impulses of Spiritual Science. Christian Esotericism in the Light of New Spirit-Knowledge
CW 97 The Christian Mystery
CW 98 Nature Beings and Spirit Beings – Their Effects in Our Visible World
CW 99 The Theosophy of the Rosicrucians
CW 100 Human Development and Christ-Knowledge
CW 101 Myths and Legends. Occult Signs and Symbols
CW 102 The Working into Human Beings by Spiritual Beings
CW 103 The Gospel of John
CW 104 The Apocalypse of John
CW 104a From the Picture-Script of the Apocalypse of John
CW 105 Universe, Earth, the Human Being: Their Being and Development, as well as Their Reflection in the Connection between Egyptian Mythology and Modern Culture
CW 106 Egyptian Myths and Mysteries in Relation to the Active Spiritual Forces of the Present
CW 107 Spiritual-Scientific Knowledge of the Human Being
CW 108 Answering the Questions of Life and the World through Anthroposophy

CW 109 The Principle of Spiritual Economy in Connection with the Question of Reincarnation. An Aspect of the Spiritual Guidance of Humanity
CW 110 The Spiritual Hierarchies and Their Reflection in the Physical World. Zodiac, Planets and Cosmos
CW 111 Contained in 109
CW 112 The Gospel of John in Relation to the Three Other Gospels, Especially the Gospel of Luke
CW 113 The Orient in the Light of the Occident. The Children of Lucifer and the Brothers of Christ
CW 114 The Gospel of Luke
CW 115 Anthroposophy – Psychosophy – Pneumatosophy
CW 116 The Christ-Impulse and the Development of "I"- Consciousness
CW 117 The Deeper Secrets of the Development of Humanity in Light of the Gospels
CW 118 The Event of the Christ-Appearance in the Etheric World
CW 119 Macrocosm and Microcosm. The Large World and the Small World. Soul-Questions, Life-Questions, Spirit-Questions
CW 120 The Revelation of Karma
CW 121 The Mission of Individual Folk-Souls in Connection with Germanic-Nordic Mythology
CW 122 The Secrets of the Biblical Creation-Story. The Six-Day Work in the First Book of Moses
CW 123 The Gospel of Matthew
CW 124 Excursus in the Area of the Gospel of Mark
CW 125 Paths and Goals of the Spiritual Human Being. Life Questions in the Light of Spiritual Science
CW 126 Occult History. Esoteric Observations of the Karmic Relationships of Personalities and Events of World History
CW 127 The Mission of the New Spiritual Revelation. The Christ-Event as the Middle-Point of Earth Evolution
CW 128 An Occult Physiology
CW 129 Wonders of the World, Trials of the Soul, and Revelations of the Spirit
CW 130 Esoteric Christianity and the Spiritual Guidance of Humanity
CW 131 From Jesus to Christ
CW 132 Evolution from the View Point of the Truth
CW 133 The Earthly and the Cosmic Human Being
CW 134 The World of the Senses and the World of the Spirit
CW 135 Reincarnation and Karma and their Meaning for the Culture of the Present
CW 136 The Spiritual Beings in Celestial Bodies and the Realms of Nature

| | |
|---|---|
| CW 137 | The Human Being in the Light of Occultism, Theosophy and Philosophy |
| CW 138 | On Initiation. On Eternity and the Passing Moment. On the Light of the Spirit and the Darkness of Life |
| CW 139 | The Gospel of Mark |
| CW 140 | Occult Investigation into the Life between Death and New Birth. The Living Interaction between Life and Death |
| CW 141 | Life between Death and New Birth in Relationship to Cosmic Facts |
| CW 142 | The Bhagavad Gita and the Letters of Paul |
| CW 143 | Experiences of the Supersensible. Three Paths of the Soul to Christ |
| CW 144 | The Mysteries of the East and of Christianity |
| CW 145 | What Significance Does Occult Development of the Human Being Have for His Sheaths–Physical Body, Etheric Body, Astral Body, and Self? |
| CW 146 | The Occult Foundations of the Bhagavad Gita |
| CW 147 | The Secrets of the Threshold |
| CW 148 | Out of Research in the Akasha: The Fifth Gospel |
| CW 149 | Christ and the Spiritual World. Concerning the Search for the Holy Grail |
| CW 150 | The World of the Spirit and Its Extension into Physical Existence; The Influence of the Dead in the World of the Living |
| CW 151 | Human Thought and Cosmic Thought |
| CW 152 | Preliminary Stages to the Mystery of Golgotha |
| CW 153 | The Inner Being of the Human Being and Life Between Death and New Birth |
| CW 154 | How does One Gain an Understanding of the Spiritual World? The Flowing in of Spiritual Impulses from out of the World of the Deceased |
| CW 155 | Christ and the Human Soul. Concerning the Meaning of Life. Theosophical Morality. Anthroposophy and Christianity |
| CW 156 | Occult Reading and Occult Hearing |
| CW 157 | Human Destinies and the Destiny of Peoples |
| CW 157a | The Formation of Destiny and the Life after Death |
| CW 158 | The Connection Between the Human Being and the Elemental World. Kalevala – Olaf Asteson – The Russian People – The World as the Result of the Influences of Equilibrium |
| CW 159 | The Mystery of Death. The Nature and Significance of Middle Europe and the European Folk Spirits |
| CW 160 | In CW 159 |
| CW 161 | Paths of Spiritual Knowledge and the Renewal of the Artistic Worldview |
| CW 162 | Questions of Art and Life in Light of Spiritual Science |

CW 163 Coincidence, Necessity and Providence. Imaginative Knowledge and the Processes after Death
CW 164 The Value of Thinking for a Knowledge That Satisfies the Human Being. The Relationship of Spiritual Science to Natural Science
CW 165 The Spiritual Unification of Humanity through the Christ-Impulse
CW 166 Necessity and Freedom in the Events of the World and in Human Action
CW 167 The Present and the Past in the Human Spirit
CW 168 The Connection between the Living and the Dead
CW 169 World-being and Selfhood
CW 170 The Riddle of the Human Being. The Spiritual Background of Human History. Cosmic and Human History, Vol. 1
CW 171 Inner Development-Impulses of Humanity. Goethe and the Crisis of the 19th Century. Cosmic and Human History, Vol. 2
CW 172 The Karma of the Vocation of the Human Being in Connection with Goethe's Life. Cosmic and Human History, Vol. 3
CW 173 Contemporary-Historical Considerations: The Karma of Untruthfulness, Part One. Cosmic and Human History, Vol. 4
CW 174 Contemporary-Historical Considerations: The Karma of Untruthfulness, Part Two. Cosmic and Human History, Vol. 5
CW 174a Middle Europe between East and West. Cosmic and Human History, Vol. 6
CW 174b The Spiritual Background of the First World War. Cosmic and Human History, Vol. 7
CW 175 Building Stones for an Understanding of the Mystery of Golgotha. Cosmic and Human Metamorphoses
CW 176 Truths of Evolution of the Individual and Humanity. The Karma of Materialism
CW 177 The Spiritual Background of the Outer World. The Fall of the Spirits of Darkness. Spiritual Beings and Their Effects, Vol. 1
CW 178 Individual Spiritual Beings and their Influence in the Soul of the Human Being. Spiritual Beings and their Effects, Vol. 2
CW 179 Spiritual Beings and Their Effects. Historical Necessity and Freedom. The Influences on Destiny from out of the World of the Dead. Spiritual Beings and Their Effects, Vol. 3
CW 180 Mystery Truths and Christmas Impulses. Ancient Myths and their Meaning. Spiritual Beings and Their Effects, Vol. 4
CW 181 Earthly Death and Cosmic Life. Anthroposophical Gifts for Life. Necessities of Consciousness for the Present and the Future.
CW 182 Death as Transformation of Life
CW 183 The Science of the Development of the Human Being
CW 184 The Polarity of Duration and Development in Human Life. The Cosmic Pre-History of Humanity

| | |
|---|---|
| CW 185 | Historical Symptomology |
| CW 185a | Historical-Developmental Foundations for Forming a Social Judgment |
| CW 186 | The Fundamental Social Demands of Our Time–In Changed Situations |
| CW 187 | How Can Humanity Find the Christ Again? The Threefold Shadow-Existence of our Time and the New Christ-Light |
| CW 188 | Goetheanism, a Transformation-Impulse and Resurrection-Thought. Science of the Human Being and Science of Sociology |
| CW 189 | The Social Question as a Question of Consciousness. The Spiritual Background of the Social Question, Vol. 1 |
| CW 190 | Impulses of the Past and the Future in Social Occurrences. The Spiritual Background of the Social Question, Vol. 2 |
| CW 191 | Social Understanding from Spiritual-Scientific Cognition. The Spiritual Background of the Social Question, Vol. 3 |
| CW 192 | Spiritual-Scientific Treatment of Social and Pedagogical Questions |
| CW 193 | The Inner Aspect of the Social Riddle. Luciferic Past and Ahrimanic Future |
| CW 194 | The Mission of Michael. The Revelation of the Actual Mysteries of the Human Being |
| CW 195 | Cosmic New Year and the New Year Idea |
| CW 196 | Spiritual and Social Transformations in the Development of Humanity |
| CW 197 | Polarities in the Development of Humanity: West and East Materialism and Mysticism Knowledge and Belief |
| CW 198 | Healing Factors for the Social Organism |
| CW 199 | Spiritual Science as Knowledge of the Foundational Impulses of Social Formation |
| CW 200 | The New Spirituality and the Christ-Experience of the 20th Century |
| CW 201 | The Correspondences Between Microcosm and Macrocosm. The Human Being – A Hieroglyph of the Universe. The Human Being in Relationship with the Cosmos: 1 |
| CW 202 | The Bridge between the World-Spirituality and the Physical Aspect of the Human Being. The Search for the New Isis, the Divine Sophia. The Human Being in Relationship with the Cosmos: 2 |
| CW 203 | The Responsibility of Human Beings for the Development of the World through their Spiritual Connection with the Planet Earth and the World of the Stars. The Human Being in Relationship with the Cosmos: 3 |
| CW 204 | Perspectives of the Development of Humanity. The Materialistic Knowledge-Impulse and the Task of Anthroposophy. The Human Being in Relationship with the Cosmos: 4 |

CW 205 Human Development, World-Soul, and World-Spirit. Part One: The Human Being as a Being of Body and Soul in Relationship to the World. The Human Being in Relationship with the Cosmos: 5
CW 206 Human Development, World-Soul, and World-Spirit. Part Two: The Human Being as a Spiritual Being in the Process of Historical Development. The Human Being in Relationship with the Cosmos: 6
CW 207 Anthroposophy as Cosmosophy. Part One: Characteristic Features of the Human Being in the Earthly and the Cosmic Realms. The Human Being in Relationship with the Cosmos: 7
CW 208 Anthroposophy as Cosmosophy. Part Two: The Forming of the Human Being as the Result of Cosmic Influence. The Human Being in Relationship with the Cosmos: 8
CW 209 Nordic and Central European Spiritual Impulses. The Festival of the Appearance of Christ. The Human Being in Relationship with the Cosmos: 9
CW 210 Old and New Methods of Initiation. Drama and Poetry in the Change of Consciousness in the Modern Age
CW 211 The Sun Mystery and the Mystery of Death and Resurrection. Exoteric and Esoteric Christianity
CW 212 Human Soul Life and Spiritual Striving in Connection with World and Earth Development
CW 213 Human Questions and World Answers
CW 214 The Mystery of the Trinity: The Human Being in Relationship to the Spiritual World in the Course of Time
CW 215 Philosophy, Cosmology, and Religion in Anthroposophy
CW 216 The Fundamental Impulses of the World-Historical Development of Humanity
CW 217 Spiritually Active Forces in the Coexistence of the Older and Younger Generations. Pedagogical Course for Youth
CW 217a Youth's Cognitive Task
CW 218 Spiritual Connections in the Forming of the Human Organism
CW 219 The Relationship of the World of the Stars to the Human Being, and of the Human Being to the World of the Stars. The Spiritual Communion of Humanity
CW 220 Living Knowledge of Nature. Intellectual Fall and Spiritual Redemption
CW 221 Earth-Knowing and Heaven-Insight
CW 222 The Imparting of Impulses to World-Historical Events through Spiritual Powers
CW 223 The Cycle of the Year as Breathing Process of the Earth and the Four Great Festival-Seasons. Anthroposophy and Human Heart (Gemüt)

CW 224 The Human Soul and its Connection with Divine-Spiritual Individualities. The Internalization of the Festivals of the Year
CW 225 Three Perspectives of Anthroposophy. Cultural Phenomena observed from a Spiritual-Scientific Perspective
CW 226 Human Being, Human Destiny, and World Development
CW 227 Initiation-Knowledge
CW 228 Science of Initiation and Knowledge of the Stars. The Human Being in the Past, the Present, and the Future from the Viewpoint of the Development of Consciousness
CW 229 The Experiencing of the Course of the Year in Four Cosmic Imaginations
CW 230 The Human Being as Harmony of the Creative, Building, and Formative World-Word
CW 231 The Supersensible Human Being, Understood Anthroposophically
CW 232 The Forming of the Mysteries
CW 233 World History Illuminated by Anthroposophy and as the Foundation for Knowledge of the Human Spirit
CW 233a Mystery Sites of the Middle Ages: Rosicrucianism and the Modern Initiation-Principle. The Festival of Easter as Part of the History of the Mysteries of Humanity
CW 234 Anthroposophy. A Summary after 21 Years
CW 235 Esoteric Observations of Karmic Relationships in 6 Volumes, Vol. 1
CW 236 Esoteric Observations of Karmic Relationships in 6 Volumes, Vol. 2
CW 237 Esoteric Observations of Karmic Relationships in 6 Volumes, Vol. 3: The Karmic Relationships of the Anthroposophical Movement
CW 238 Esoteric Observations of Karmic Relationships in 6 Volumes, Vol. 4: The Spiritual Life of the Present in Relationship to the Anthroposophical Movement
CW 239 Esoteric Observations of Karmic Relationships in 6 Volumes, Vol. 5
CW 240 Esoteric Observations of Karmic Relationships in 6 Volumes, Vol. 6
CW 243 The Consciousness of the Initiate
CW 245 Instructions for an Esoteric Schooling
CW 250 The Building-Up of the Anthroposophical Society. From the Beginning to the Outbreak of the First World War
CW 251 The History of the Goetheanum Building-Association
CW 252 Life in the Anthroposophical Society from the First World War to the Burning of the First Goetheanum
CW 253 The Problems of Living Together in the Anthroposophical Society. On the Dornach Crisis of 1915. With Highlights on Swedenborg's Clairvoyance, the Views of Freudian Psychoanalysts, and the Concept of Love in Relation to Mysticism

CW 254 The Occult Movement in the 19th Century and Its Relationship to World Culture. Significant Points from the Exoteric Cultural Life around the Middle of the 19th Century
CW 255 Rudolf Steiner during the First World War
CW 255a Anthroposophy and the Reformation of Society. On the History of the Threefold Movement
CW 255b Anthroposophy and Its Opponents, 1919-1921
CW 256 How Can the Anthroposophical Movement Be Financed?
CW 256a Futurum, Inc. / International Laboratories, Inc.
CW 256b The Coming Day, Inc.
CW 257 Anthroposophical Community-Building
CW 258 The History of and Conditions for the Anthroposophical Movement in Relationship to the Anthroposophical Society. A Stimulus to Self-Contemplation
CW 259 The Year of Destiny 1923 in the History of the Anthroposophical Society. From the Burning of the Goetheanum to the Christmas Conference
CW 260 The Christmas Conference for the Founding of the General Anthroposophical Society
CW 260a The Constitution of the General Anthroposophical Society and the School for Spiritual Science. The Rebuilding of the Goetheanum
CW 261 Our Dead. Addresses, Words of Remembrance, and Meditative Verses, 1906-1924
CW 262 Rudolf Steiner and Marie Steiner-von Sivers: Correspondence and Documents, 1901-1925
CW 263/1 Rudolf Steiner and Edith Maryon: Correspondence: Letters, Verses, Sketches, 1912-1924
CW 264 On the History and the Contents of the First Section of the Esoteric School from 1904 to 1914. Letters, Newsletters, Documents, Lectures
CW 265 On the History and Out of the Contents of the Ritual-Knowledge Section of the Esoteric School from 1904 to 1914. Documents, and Lectures from the Years 1906 to 1914, as well as on New Approaches to Ritual-Knowledge Work in the Years 1921-1924
CW 266/1 From the Contents of the Esoteric Lessons. Volume 1: 1904-1909. Notes from Memory of Participants. Meditation texts from the notes of Rudolf Steiner
CW 266/2 From the Contents of the Esoteric Lessons. Volume 2: 1910-1912. Notes from Memory of Participants
CW 266/3 From the Contents of the Esoteric Lessons. Volume 3: 1913, 1914 and 1920-1923. Notes from Memory of Participants. Meditation texts from the notes of Rudolf Steiner

CW 267 Soul-Exercises: Vol. 1: Exercises with Word and Image Meditations for the Methodological Development of Higher Powers of Knowledge, 1904-1924
CW 268 Soul-Exercises: Vol. 2: Mantric Verses, 1903-1925
CW 269 Ritual Texts for the Celebration of the Free Christian Religious Instruction. The Collected Verses for Teachers and Students of the Waldorf School
CW 270 Esoteric Instructions for the First Class of the School for Spiritual Science at the Goetheanum 1924, 4 Volumes
CW 271 Art and Knowledge of Art. Foundations of a New Aesthetic
CW 272 Spiritual-Scientific Commentary on Goethe's "Faust" in Two Volumes. Vol. 1: Faust, the Striving Human Being
CW 273 Spiritual-Scientific Commentary on Goethe's "Faust" in Two Volumes. Vol. 2: The Faust-Problem
CW 274 Addresses for the Christmas Plays from the Old Folk Traditions
CW 275 Art in the Light of Mystery-Wisdom
CW 276 The Artistic in Its Mission in the World. The Genius of Language. The World of the Self-Revealing Radiant Appearances – Anthroposophy and Art. Anthroposophy and Poetry
CW 277 Eurythmy. The Revelation of the Speaking Soul
CW 277a The Origin and Development of Eurythmy
CW 278 Eurythmy as Visible Song
CW 279 Eurythmy as Visible Speech
CW 280 The Method and Nature of Speech Formation
CW 281 The Art of Recitation and Declamation
CW 282 Speech Formation and Dramatic Art
CW 283 The Nature of Things Musical and the Experience of Tone in the Human Being
CW284/285 Images of Occult Seals and Pillars. The Munich Congress of Whitsun 1907 and Its Consequences
CW 286 Paths to a New Style of Architecture. "And the Building Becomes Human"
CW 287 The Building at Dornach as a Symbol of Historical Becoming and an Artistic Transformation Impulse
CW 288 Style-Forms in the Living Organic
CW 289 The Building-Idea of the Goetheanum: Lectures with Slides from the Years 1920-1921
CW 290 The Building-Idea of the Goetheanum: Lectures with Slides from the Years 1920-1921
CW 291 The Nature of Colors
CW 291a Knowledge of Colors. Supplementary Volume to "The Nature of Colors"
CW 292 Art History as Image of Inner Spiritual Impulses

CW 293 General Knowledge of the Human Being as the Foundation of Pedagogy
CW 294 The Art of Education, Methodology and Didactics
CW 295 The Art of Education: Seminar Discussions and Lectures on Lesson Planning
CW 296 The Question of Education as a Social Question
CW 297 The Idea and Practice of the Waldorf School
CW 297a Education for Life: Self-Education and the Practice of Pedagogy
CW 298 Rudolf Steiner in the Waldorf School
CW 299 Spiritual-Scientific Observations on Speech
CW 300a Conferences with the Teachers of the Free Waldorf School in Stuttgart, 1919 to 1924, in 3 Volumes, Vol. 1
CW 300b Conferences with the Teachers of the Free Waldorf School in Stuttgart, 1919 to 1924, in 3 Volumes, Vol. 2
CW 300c Conferences with the Teachers of the Free Waldorf School in Stuttgart, 1919 to 1924, in 3 Volumes, Vol. 3
CW 301 The Renewal of the Pedagogical-Didactical Art through Spiritual Science
CW 302 Knowledge of the Human Being and the Forming of Class Lessons
CW 302a Education and Teaching out of a Knowledge of the Human Being
CW 303 The Healthy Development of the Human Being
CW 304 Methods of Education and Teaching Based on Anthroposophy
CW 304a Anthroposophical Knowledge of the Human Being and Pedagogy
CW 305 The Soul-Spiritual Foundational Forces of the Art of Education. Spiritual Values in Education and Social Life
CW 306 Pedagogical Praxis from the Viewpoint of a Spiritual-Scientific Knowledge of the Human Being. The Education of the Child and Young Human Beings
CW 307 The Spiritual Life of the Present and Education
CW 308 The Method of Teaching and the Life-Requirements for Teaching
CW 309 Anthroposophical Pedagogy and Its Prerequisites
CW 310 The Pedagogical Value of a Knowledge of the Human Being and the Cultural Value of Pedagogy
CW 311 The Art of Education Out of an Understanding of the Being of Humanity
CW 312 Spiritual Science and Medicine
CW 313 Spiritual-Scientific Viewpoints on Therapy
CW 314 Physiology and Therapy Based on Spiritual Science
CW 315 Curative Eurythmy
CW 316 Meditative Observations and Instructions for a Deepening of the Art of Healing
CW 317 The Curative Education Course
CW 318 The Working Together of Doctors and Pastors

CW 319 Anthroposophical Knowledge of the Human Being and Medicine
CW 320 Spiritual-Scientific Impulses for the Development of Physics 1: The First Natural-Scientific Course: Light, Color, Tone, Mass, Electricity, Magnetism
CW 321 Spiritual-Scientific Impulses for the Development of Physics 2: The Second Natural-Scientific Course: Warmth at the Border of Positive and Negative Materiality
CW 322 The Borders of the Knowledge of Nature
CW 323 The Relationship of the various Natural-Scientific Fields to Astronomy
CW 324 Nature Observation, Mathematics, and Scientific Experimentation and Results from the Viewpoint of Anthroposophy
CW 324a The Fourth Dimension in Mathematics and Reality
CW 325 Natural Science and the World-Historical Development of Humanity since Ancient Times
CW 326 The Moment of the Coming Into Being of Natural Science in World History and Its Development Since Then
CW 327 Spiritual-Scientific Foundations for Success in Farming. The Agricultural Course
CW 328 The Social Question
CW 329 The Liberation of the Human Being as the Foundation for a New Social Form
CW 330 The Renewal of the Social Organism
CW 331 Work-Council and Socialization
CW 332 The Alliance for Threefolding and the Total Reform of Society. The Council on Culture and the Liberation of the Spiritual Life
CW 332a The Social Future
CW 333 Freedom of Thought and Social Forces
CW 334 From the Unified State to the Threefold Social Organism
CW 335 The Crisis of the Present and the Path to Healthy Thinking
CW 336 The Great Questions of the Times and Anthroposophical Spiritual Knowledge
CW 337a Social Ideas, Social Reality, Social Practice, Vol. 1: Question-and- Answer Evenings and Study Evenings of the Alliance for the Threefold Social Organism in Stuttgart, 1919-1920
CW 337b Social Ideas, Social Realities, Social Practice, Vol. 2: Discussion Evenings of the Swiss Alliance for the Threefold Social Organism
CW 338 How Does One Work on Behalf of the Impulse for the Threefold Social Organism?
CW 339 Anthroposophy, Threefold Social Organism, and the Art of Public Speaking
CW 340 The National-Economics Course. The Tasks of a New Science of Economics, Volume 1

CW 341 The National-Economics Seminar. The Tasks of a New Science of Economics, Volume 2
CW 342 Lectures and Courses on Christian Religious Work, Vol. 1: Anthroposophical Foundations for a Renewed Christian Religious Working
CW 343 Lectures and Courses on Christian Religious Work, Vol. 2: Spiritual Knowledge – Religious Feeling – Cultic Doing
CW 344 Lectures and Courses on Christian Religious Work, Vol. 3: Lectures at the Founding of the Christian Community
CW 345 Lectures and Courses on Christian Religious Work, Vol. 4: Concerning the Nature of the Working Word
CW 346 Lectures and Courses on Christian Religious Work, Vol. 5: The Apocalypse and the Working of the Priest
CW 347 The Knowledge of the Nature of the Human Being According to Body, Soul and Spirit. On Earlier Conditions of the Earth
CW 348 On Health and Illness. Foundations of a Spiritual-Scientific Doctrine of the Senses
CW 349 On the Life of the Human Being and of the Earth. On the Nature of Christianity
CW 350 Rhythms in the Cosmos and in the Human Being. How Does One Come To See the Spiritual World?
CW 351 The Human Being and the World. The Influence of the Spirit in Nature. On the Nature of Bees
CW 352 Nature and the Human Being Observed Spiritual-Scientifically
CW 353 The History of Humanity and the World-Views of the Folk Cultures
CW 354 The Creation of the World and the Human Being. Life on Earth and the Influence of the Stars

# SIGNIFICANT EVENTS IN THE LIFE OF RUDOLF STEINER

1829: June 23: birth of Johann Steiner (1829-1910)—Rudolf Steiner's father—in Geras, Lower Austria.

1834: May 8: birth of Franciska Blie (1834-1918)—Rudolf Steiner's mother—in Horn, Lower Austria. "My father and mother were both children of the glorious Lower Austrian forest district north of the Danube."

1860: May 16: marriage of Johann Steiner and Franciska Blie.

1861: February 25: birth of *Rudolf Joseph Lorenz Steiner* in Kraljevec, Croatia, near the border with Hungary, where Johann Steiner works as a telegrapher for the South Austria Railroad. Rudolf Steiner is baptized two days later, February 27, the date usually given as his birthday.

1862: Summer: the family moves to Mödling, Lower Austria.

1863: The family moves to Pottschach, Lower Austria, near the Styrian border, where Johann Steiner becomes stationmaster. "The view stretched to the mountains...majestic peaks in the distance and the sweet charm of nature in the immediate surroundings."

1864: November 15: birth of Rudolf Steiner's sister, Leopoldine (d. November 1, 1927). She will become a seamstress and live with her parents for the rest of her life.

1866: July 28: birth of Rudolf Steiner's deaf-mute brother, Gustav (d. May 1, 1941).

1867: Rudolf Steiner enters the village school. Following a disagreement between his father and the schoolmaster, whose wife falsely accused the boy of causing a commotion, Rudolf Steiner is taken out of school and taught at home.

1868: A critical experience. Unknown to the family, an aunt dies in a distant town. Sitting in the station waiting room, Rudolf Steiner sees her "form," which speaks to him, asking for help. "Beginning with this experience, a new soul life began in the boy, one in which not only the outer trees and mountains spoke to him, but also the worlds that lay behind them. From this moment on, the boy began to live with the spirits of nature...."

1869: The family moves to the peaceful, rural village of Neudorfl, near Wiener-Neustadt now in present-day Austria, where Rudolf Steiner attends the village school. Because of the "unorthodoxy" of his writing and spelling, he has to do "extra lessons."

1870: Through a book lent to him by his tutor, he discovers geometry: "To grasp something purely in the spirit brought me inner happiness. I know that I first learned happiness through geometry." The same tutor allows him to draw, while other students still struggle with their reading and writing. "An artistic element" thus enters his education.

1871: Though his parents are not religious, Rudolf Steiner becomes a "church child," a favorite of the priest, who was "an exceptional character." "Up to the age of ten or eleven, among those I came to know, he was far and away the most significant." Among other things, he introduces Steiner to Copernican, heliocentric cosmology. As an altar boy, Rudolf Steiner serves at Masses, funerals, and Corpus Christi processions. At year's end, after an incident in which he escapes a thrashing, his father forbids him to go to church.

1872: Rudolf Steiner transfers to grammar school in Wiener-Neustadt, a five-mile walk from home, which must be done in all weathers.

1873-75: Through his teachers and on his own, Rudolf Steiner has many wonderful experiences with science and mathematics. Outside school, he teaches himself analytic geometry, trigonometry, differential equations, and calculus.

1876: Rudolf Steiner begins tutoring other students. He learns bookbinding from his father. He also teaches himself stenography.

1877: Rudolf Steiner discovers Kant's *Critique of Pure Reason*, which he reads and rereads. He also discovers and reads von Rotteck's *World History*.

1878: He studies extensively in contemporary psychology and philosophy.

1879: Rudolf Steiner graduates from high school with honors. His father is transferred to Inzersdorf, near Vienna. He uses his first visit to Vienna "to purchase a great number of philosophy books"— Kant, Fichte, Schelling, and Hegel, as well as numerous histories of philosophy. His aim: to find a path from the "I" to nature.

October 1879-1883: Rudolf Steiner attends the Technical College in Vienna—to study mathematics, chemistry, physics, mineralogy, botany, zoology, biology, geology, and mechanics—with a scholarship. He also attends lectures in history and literature, while avidly reading philosophy on his own. His two favorite professors are Karl Julius Schröer (German language and literature) and Edmund Reitlinger (physics). He also audits lectures by Robert Zimmerman on aesthetics and Franz Brentano on philosophy. During this year he begins his friendship with Moritz Zitter (1861-1921), who will help support him financially when he is in Berlin.

1880: Rudolf Steiner attends lectures on Schiller and Goethe by Karl Julius Schröer, who becomes his mentor. Also "through a remarkable combination of circumstances," he meets Felix Koguzki, an "herb gatherer" and healer, who could "see deeply into the secrets of nature." Rudolf Steiner will meet and study with this "emissary of the Master" throughout his time in Vienna.

1881: January: "... I didn't sleep a wink. I was busy with philosophical problems until about 12:30 a.m. Then, finally, I threw myself down on my couch. All my striving during the previous year had been to research whether the following statement by Schelling was true or not: *Within everyone dwells a secret, marvelous capacity to draw back from the stream of time—out of the self clothed in all that comes to us from outside—into our innermost being and there, in the immutable form of the Eternal, to look into ourselves.* I believe, and I am still quite certain of it, that I discovered this capacity in myself; I had long had an inkling of it. Now the whole of idealist philosophy stood before me in modified form. What's a sleepless night compared to that!"

Rudolf Steiner begins communicating with leading thinkers of the day, who send him books in return, which he reads eagerly.

July: "I am not one of those who dives into the day like an animal in human form. I pursue a quite specific goal, an idealistic aim—knowledge of the truth! This cannot be done offhandedly. It requires the greatest striving in the world, free of all egotism, and equally of all resignation."

August: Steiner puts down on paper for the first time thoughts for a "Philosophy of Freedom." "The striving for the absolute: this human yearning is freedom." He also seeks to outline a "peasant philosophy," describing what the worldview of a "peasant"—one who lives close to the earth and the old ways—really is.

1881-1882: Felix Koguzki, the herb gatherer, reveals himself to be the envoy of another, higher initiatory personality, who instructs Rudolf Steiner to penetrate Fichte's philosophy and to master modern scientific thinking as a preparation for right entry into the spirit. This "Master" also teaches him the double (evolutionary and involutionary) nature of time.

1882: Through the offices of Karl Julius Schröer, Rudolf Steiner is asked by Joseph Kurschner to edit Goethe's scientific works for the *Deutschen National-Literatur* edition. He writes "A Possible Critique of Atomistic Concepts" and sends it to Friedrich Theodore Vischer.

1883: Rudolf Steiner completes his college studies and begins work on the Goethe project.

1884: First volume of Goethe's *Scientific Writings* (CW 1) appears (March). He lectures on Goethe and Lessing, and Goethe's approach to science. In July, he enters the household of Ladislaus and Pauline Specht as tutor to the four Specht boys. He will live there until 1890. At this time, he meets Josef Breuer (1842-1925), the coauthor with Sigmund Freud of *Studies in Hysteria*, who is the Specht family doctor.

1885: While continuing to edit Goethe's writings, Rudolf Steiner reads deeply in contemporary philosophy (Edouard von Hartmann, Johannes Volkelt, and Richard Wahle, among others).

1886: May: Rudolf Steiner sends Kurschner the manuscript of *Outlines of Goethe's Theory of Knowledge* (CW 2), which appears in October, and which he sends out widely. He also meets the poet Marie Eugenie Delle Grazie and writes "Nature and Our Ideals" for her. He attends her salon, where he meets many priests, theologians, and philosophers, who will become his friends. Meanwhile, the director of the Goethe Archive in Weimar requests his collaboration with the *Sophien* edition of Goethe's works, particularly the writings on color.

1887: At the beginning of the year, Rudolf Steiner is very sick. As the year progresses and his health improves, he becomes increasingly "a man of letters," lecturing, writing essays, and taking part in Austrian cultural life. In August-September, the second volume of Goethe's *Scientific Writings* appears.

1888: January-July: Rudolf Steiner assumes editorship of the "German Weekly" (*Deutsche Wochenschrift*). He begins lecturing more intensively, giving, for example, a lecture titled "Goethe as Father of a New Aesthetics." He meets and becomes soul friends with Friedrich Eckstein (1861-1939), a vegetarian, philosopher of symbolism, alchemist, and musician, who will introduce him to various spiritual currents (including Theosophy) and with whom he will meditate and interpret esoteric and alchemical texts.

1889: Rudolf Steiner first reads Nietzsche (*Beyond Good and Evil*). He encounters Theosophy again and learns of Madame Blavatsky in the Theosophical circle around Marie Lang (1858-1934). Here he also meets well-known figures of Austrian life, as well as esoteric figures like the occultist Franz Hartman and Karl Leinigen-Billigen (translator of C.G. Harrison's *The Transcendental Universe*.) During this period, Steiner first reads A.P. Sinnett's *Esoteric Buddhism* and Mabel Collins's *Light on the Path*. He also begins traveling, visiting Budapest, Weimar, and Berlin (where he meets philosopher Edouard von Hartman).

1890: Rudolf Steiner finishes volume 3 of Goethe's scientific writings. He begins his doctoral dissertation, which will become *Truth and Science* (CW 3). He also meets the poet and feminist Rosa Mayreder (1858-1938), with whom he can exchange his most intimate thoughts. In September, Rudolf Steiner moves to Weimar to work in the Goethe-Schiller Archive.

1891: Volume 3 of the Kurschner edition of Goethe appears. Meanwhile, Rudolf Steiner edits Goethe's studies in mineralogy and scientific writings for the *Sophien* edition. He meets Ludwig Laistner of the Cotta Publishing Company, who asks for a book on the basic question of metaphysics. From this will result, ultimately, *The Philosophy of Freedom* (CW 4), which will be published not by Cotta but by Emil Felber. In October, Rudolf Steiner takes the oral exam for a doctorate in philosophy, mathematics, and mechanics at Rostock University, receiving his doctorate on the twenty-sixth. In November, he gives his first lecture on Goethe's "Fairy Tale" in Vienna.

1892: Rudolf Steiner continues work at the Goethe-Schiller Archive and on his *Philosophy of Freedom*. *Truth and Science*, his doctoral dissertation, is published. Steiner undertakes to write introductions to books on Schopenhauer and Jean Paul for Cotta. At year's end, he finds lodging with Anna Eunike, née Schulz (1853-1911), a widow with four daughters and a son. He also develops a friendship with Otto Erich Hartleben (1864-1905) with whom he shares literary interests.

1893: Rudolf Steiner begins his habit of producing many reviews and articles. In March, he gives a lecture titled "Hypnotism, with Reference to Spiritism." In September, volume 4 of the Kurschner edition is completed. In November, *The Philosophy of Freedom* appears. This year, too, he meets John Henry Mackay (1864-1933), the anarchist, and Max Stirner, a scholar and biographer.

1894: Rudolf Steiner meets Elisabeth Förster Nietzsche, the philosopher's sister, and begins to read Nietzsche in earnest, beginning with the as yet unpublished *Antichrist.* He also meets Ernst Haeckel (1834-1919). In the fall, he begins to write *Nietzsche, A Fighter against His Time* (CW 5).

1895: May, *Nietzsche, A Fighter against His Time* appears.

1896: January 22: Rudolf Steiner sees Friedrich Nietzsche for the first and only time. Moves between the Nietzsche and the Goethe-Schiller Archives, where he completes his work before year's end. He falls out with Elisabeth Förster Nietzsche, thus ending his association with the Nietzsche Archive.

1897: Rudolf Steiner finishes the manuscript of *Goethe's Worldview* (CW 6). He moves to Berlin with Anna Eunike and begins editorship of the *Magazin fur Literatur.* From now on, Steiner will write countless reviews, literary and philosophical articles, and so on. He begins lecturing at the "Free Literary Society." In September, he attends the Zionist Congress in Basel. He sides with Dreyfus in the Dreyfus affair.

1898: Rudolf Steiner is very active as an editor in the political, artistic, and theatrical life of Berlin. He becomes friendly with John Henry Mackay and poet Ludwig Jacobowski (1868-1900). He joins Jacobowski's circle of writers, artists, and scientists—"The Coming Ones" (*Die Kommenden*)—and contributes lectures to the group until 1903. He also lectures at the "League for College Pedagogy." He writes an article for Goethe's sesquicentennial, "Goethe's Secret Revelation," on the "Fairy Tale of the Green Snake and the Beautiful Lily."

1898-99: "This was a trying time for my soul as I looked at Christianity.... ...I was able to progress only by contemplating, by means of spiritual perception, the evolution of Christianity . . . . Conscious knowledge of real Christianity began to dawn in me around the turn of the century. This seed continued to develop. My soul trial occurred shortly before the beginning of the twentieth century. It was decisive for my soul's development that I stood spiritually before the Mystery of Golgotha in a deep and solemn celebration of knowledge."

1899: Rudolf Steiner begins teaching and giving lectures and lecture cycles at the Workers' College, founded by Wilhelm Liebknecht (1826-1900). He will continue to do so until 1904. Writes: *Literature and Spiritual Life in the Nineteenth Century; Individualism in Philosophy*; *Haeckel and His Opponents; Poetry in the Present;* and begins what will become (fifteen years later). *The Riddles of Philosophy* (CW 18). He also meets many artists and writers, including Käthe Kollwitz, Stefan

Zweig, and Rainer Maria Rilke. On October 31, he marries Anna Eunike.

1900: "I thought that the turn of the century must bring humanity a new light. It seemed to me that the separation of human thinking and willing from the spirit had peaked. A turn or reversal of direction in human evolution seemed to me a necessity." Rudolf Steiner finishes *World and Life Views in the Nineteenth Century* (the second part of what will become *The Riddles of Philosophy*) and dedicates it to Ernst Haeckel. It is published in March. He continues lecturing at *Die Kommenden*, whose leadership he assumes after the death of Jacobowski. Also, he gives the Gutenberg Jubilee lecture before 7,000 typesetters and printers. In September, Rudolf Steiner is invited by Count and Countess Brockdorff to lecture in the Theosophical Library. His first lecture is on Nietzsche. His second lecture is titled "Goethe's Secret Revelation." October 6, he begins a lecture cycle on the mystics that will become *Mystics after Modernism* (CW 7). November-December: "Marie von Sivers appears in the audience...." Also in November, Steiner gives his first lecture at the Giordano Bruno Bund (where he will continue to lecture until May, 1905). He speaks on Bruno and modern Rome, focusing on the importance of the philosophy of Thomas Aquinas as monism.

1901: In continual financial straits, Rudolf Steiner's early friends Moritz Zitter and Rosa Mayreder help support him. In October, he begins the lecture cycle *Christianity as Mystical Fact* (CW 8) at the Theosophical Library. In November, he gives his first "Theosophical lecture" on Goethe's "Fairy Tale" in Hamburg at the invitation of Wilhelm Hubbe-Schleiden. He also attends a tea to celebrate the founding of the Theosophical Society at Count and Countess Brockdorff's. He gives a lecture cycle, "From Buddha to Christ," for the circle of the *Kommenden*. November 17, Marie von Sivers asks Rudolf Steiner if Theosophy does not need a Western-Christian spiritual movement (to complement Theosophy's Eastern emphasis). "The question was posed. Now, following spiritual laws, I could begin to give an answer...." In December, Rudolf Steiner writes his first article for a Theosophical publication. At year's end, the Brockdorffs and possibly Wilhelm Hubbe-Schleiden ask Rudolf Steiner to join the Theosophical Society and undertake the leadership of the German section. Rudolf Steiner agrees, on the condition that Marie von Sivers (then in Italy) work with him.

1902: Beginning in January, Rudolf Steiner attends the opening of the Workers' School in Spandau with Rosa Luxemberg (1870-1919). January 17, Rudolf Steiner joins the Theosophical Society. In April, he is asked to become general secretary of the German Section of the Theosophical Society, and works on preparations for its founding. In July, he visits London for a Theosophical congress. He meets Bertram

Keightly, G.R.S. Mead, A.P. Sinnett, and Annie Besant, among others. In September, *Christianity as Mystical Fact* appears. In October, Rudolf Steiner gives his first public lecture on Theosophy ("Monism and Theosophy") to about three hundred people at the Giordano Bruno Bund. On October 19-21, the German Section of the Theosophical Society has its first meeting; Rudolf Steiner is the general secretary, and Annie Besant attends. Steiner lectures on practical karma studies. On October 23, Annie Besant inducts Rudolf Steiner into the Esoteric School of the Theosophical Society. On October 25, Steiner begins a weekly series of lectures: "The Field of Theosophy." During this year, Rudolf Steiner also first meets Ita Wegman (1876-1943), who will become his close collaborator in his final years.

1903: Rudolf Steiner holds about 300 lectures and seminars. In May, the first issue of the periodical *Luzifer* appears. In June, Rudolf Steiner visits London for the first meeting of the Federation of the European Sections of the Theosophical Society, where he meets Colonel Olcott. He begins to write *Theosophy* (CW 9).

1904: Rudolf Steiner continues lecturing at the Workers' College and elsewhere (about 90 lectures), while lecturing intensively all over Germany among Theosophists (about a 140 lectures). In February, he meets Carl Unger (1878-1929), who will become a member of the board of the Anthroposophical Society (1913). In March, he meets Michael Bauer (1871-1929), a Christian mystic, who will also be on the board. In May, *Theosophy* appears, with the dedication: "To the spirit of Giordano Bruno." Rudolf Steiner and Marie von Sivers visit London for meetings with Annie Besant. June: Rudolf Steiner and Marie von Sivers attend the meeting of the Federation of European Sections of the Theosophical Society in Amsterdam. In July, Steiner begins the articles in *Luzifer-Gnosis* that will become *How to Know Higher Worlds* (CW 10) and *Cosmic Memory* (CW 11). In September, Annie Besant visits Germany. In December, Steiner lectures on Freemasonry. He mentions the High Grade Masonry derived from John Yarker and represented by Theodore Reuss and Karl Kellner as a blank slate "into which a good image could be placed."

1905: This year, Steiner ends his non-Theosophical lecturing activity. Supported by Marie von Sivers, his Theosophical lecturing—both in public and in the Theosophical Society—increases significantly: "The German Theosophical Movement is of exceptional importance." Steiner recommends reading, among others, Fichte, Jacob Boehme, and Angelus Silesius. He begins to introduce Christian themes into Theosophy. He also begins to work with doctors (Felix Peipers and Ludwig Noll). In July, he is in London for the Federation of European Sections, where he attends a lecture by Annie Besant: "I have seldom seen Mrs. Besant speak in so inward and heartfelt a manner...." "Through Mrs. Besant I have found the way to H.P. Blavatsky."

September to October, he gives a course of thirty-one lectures for a small group of esoteric students. In October, the annual meeting of the German Section of the Theosophical Society, which still remains very small, takes place. Rudolf Steiner reports membership has risen from 121 to 377 members. In November, seeking to establish esoteric "continuity," Rudolf Steiner and Marie von Sivers participate in a "Memphis-Misraim" Masonic ceremony. They pay forty-five marks for membership. "Yesterday, you saw how little remains of former esoteric institutions." "We are dealing only with a 'framework'... for the present, nothing lies behind it. The occult powers have completely withdrawn."

1906: Expansion of Theosophical work. Rudolf Steiner gives about 245 lectures, only 44 of which take place in Berlin. Cycles are given in Paris, Leipzig, Stuttgart, and Munich. Esoteric work also intensifies. Rudolf Steiner begins writing *An Outline of Esoteric Science* (CW 13). In January, Rudolf Steiner receives permission (a patent) from the Great Orient of the Scottish A & A Thirty-Three Degree Rite of the Order of the Ancient Freemasons of the Memphis-Misraim Rite to direct a chapter under the name "Mystica Aeterna." This will become the "Cognitive Cultic Section" (also called "Misraim Service") of the Esoteric School. (See: *From the History and Contents of the Cognitive Cultic Section* (CW 264). During this time, Steiner also meets Albert Schweitzer. In May, he is in Paris, where he visits Edouard Schuré. Many Russians attend his lectures (including Konstantin Balmont, Dimitri Mereszkovski, Zinaida Hippius, and Maximilian Woloshin). He attends the General Meeting of the European Federation of the Theosophical Society, at which Col. Olcott is present for the last time. He spends the year's end in Venice and Rome, where he writes and works on his translation of H.P. Blavatsky's *Key to Theosophy.*

1907: Further expansion of the German Theosophical Movement according to the Rosicrucian directive to "introduce spirit into the world"—in education, in social questions, in art, and in science. In February, Col. Olcott dies in Adyar. Before he dies, Olcott indicates that "the Masters" wish Annie Besant to succeed him: much politicking ensues. Rudolf Steiner supports Besant's candidacy. April-May: preparations for the Congress of the Federation of European Sections of the Theosophical Society—the great, watershed Whitsun "Munich Congress," attended by Annie Besant and others. Steiner decides to separate Eastern and Western (Christian-Rosicrucian) esoteric schools. He takes his esoteric school out of the Theosophical Society (Besant and Rudolf Steiner are "in harmony" on this). Steiner makes his first lecture tours to Austria and Hungary. That summer, he is in Italy. In September, he visits Edouard Schuré, who will write the introduction to the French edition of *Christianity as Mystical Fact* in Barr, Alsace. Rudolf Steiner writes the autobiographical statement known as the "Barr Document." In *Luzifer–Gnosis*, "The Education of the Child" appears.

1908: The movement grows (membership: 1150). Lecturing expands. Steiner makes his first extended lecture tour to Holland and Scandinavia, as well as visits to Naples and Sicily. Themes: St. John's Gospel, the Apocalypse, Egypt, science, philosophy, and logic. *Luzifer-Gnosis* ceases publication. In Berlin, Marie von Sivers (with Johanna Mücke (1864-1949) forms the *Philosophisch-Theosophisch* (after 1915 *Philosophisch-Anthroposophisch*) *Verlag* to publish Steiner's work. Steiner gives lecture cycles titled *The Gospel of St. John* (CW 103) and *The Apocalypse* (104).

1909: *An Outline of Esoteric Science* appears. Lecturing and travel continues. Rudolf Steiner's spiritual research expands to include the polarity of Lucifer and Ahriman; the work of great individualities in history; the Maitreya Buddha and the Bodhisattvas; spiritual economy (CW 109); the work of the spiritual hierarchies in heaven and on Earth (CW 110). He also deepens and intensifies his research into the Gospels, giving lectures on the Gospel of St. Luke (CW 114) with the first mention of two Jesus children. Meets and becomes friends with Christian Morgenstern (1871-1914). In April, he lays the foundation stone for the Malsch model—the building that will lead to the first Goetheanum. In May, the International Congress of the Federation of European Sections of the Theosophical Society takes place in Budapest. Rudolf Steiner receives the Subba Row medal for *How to Know Higher Worlds*. During this time, Charles W. Leadbeater discovers Jiddu Krishnamurti (1895-1986) and proclaims him the future "world teacher," the bearer of the Maitreya Buddha and the "reappearing Christ." In October, Steiner delivers seminal lectures on "anthroposophy," which he will try, unsuccessfully, to rework over the next years into the unfinished work, *Anthroposophy (A Fragment)* (CW 45).

1910: New themes: *The Reappearance of Christ in the Etheric* (CW 118); *The Fifth Gospel; The Mission of Folk Souls* (CW 121); *Occult History* (CW 126); the evolving development of etheric cognitive capacities. Rudolf Steiner continues his Gospel research with *The Gospel of St. Matthew* (CW 123). In January, his father dies. In April, he takes a month-long trip to Italy, including Rome, Monte Cassino, and Sicily. He also visits Scandinavia again. July-August, he writes the first mystery drama, *The Portal of Initiation* (CW 14). In November, he gives "psychosophy" lectures. In December, he submits "On the Psychological Foundations and Epistemological Framework of Theosophy" to the International Philosophical Congress in Bologna.

1911: The crisis in the Theosophical Society deepens. In January, "The Order of the Rising Sun," which will soon become "The Order of the Star in the East," is founded for the coming world teacher, Krishnamurti. At the same time, Marie von Sivers, Rudolf Steiner's coworker, falls ill. Fewer lectures are given, but important new ground is broken. In Prague, in March, Steiner meets Franz Kafka (1883-1924) and Hugo Bergmann (1883-1975). In April, he delivers his paper to the

Philosophical Congress. He writes the second mystery drama, *The Soul's Probation* (CW 14). Also, while Marie von Sivers is convalescing, Rudolf Steiner begins work on *Calendar 1912/1913*, which will contain the "Calendar of the Soul" meditations. On March 19, Anna (Eunike) Steiner dies. In September, Rudolf Steiner visits Einsiedeln, birthplace of Paracelsus. In December, Friedrich Rittelmeyer, future founder of the Christian Community, meets Rudolf Steiner. The *Johannes-Bauverein*, the "building committee," which would lead to the first Goetheanum (first planned for Munich), is also founded, and a preliminary committee for the founding of an independent association is created that, in the following year, will become the Anthroposophical Society. Important lecture cycles include *Occult Physiology* (CW 128); *Wonders of the World* (CW 129); *From Jesus to Christ* (CW 131). Other themes: esoteric Christianity; Christian Rosenkreutz; the spiritual guidance of humanity; the sense world and the world of the spirit.

1912: Despite the ongoing, now increasing crisis in the Theosophical Society, much is accomplished: *Calendar 1912/1913* is published; eurythmy is created; both the third mystery drama, *The Guardian of the Threshold* (CW 14) and *A Way of Self-Knowledge* (CW 16) are written. New (or renewed) themes included life between death and rebirth and karma and reincarnation. Other lecture cycles: *Spiritual Beings in the Heavenly Bodies and the Kingdoms of Nature* (CW 136); *The Human Being in the Light of Occultism, Theosophy, and Philosophy* (CW 137); *The Gospel of St. Mark* (CW 139); and *The Bhagavad Gita and the Epistles of Paul* (CW 142). On May 8, Rudolf Steiner celebrates White Lotus Day, H.P. Blavatsky's death day, which he had faithfully observed for the past decade, for the last time. In August, Rudolf Steiner suggests the "independent association" be called the "Anthroposophical Society." In September, the first eurythmy course takes place. In October, Rudolf Steiner declines recognition of a Theosophical Society lodge dedicated to the Star of the East and decides to expel all Theosophical Society members belonging to the order. Also, with Marie von Sivers, he first visits Dornach, near Basel, Switzerland, and they stand on the hill where the Goetheanum will be. In November, a Theosophical Society lodge is opened by direct mandate from Adyar (Annie Besant). In December, a meeting of the German section occurs at which it is decided that belonging to the Order of the Star of the East is incompatible with membership in the Theosophical Society. December 28: informal founding of the Anthroposophical Society in Berlin.

1913: Expulsion of the German section from the Theosophical Society. February 2-3: Foundation meeting of the Anthroposophical Society. Board members include: Marie von Sivers, Michael Bauer, and Carl Unger. September 20: Laying of the foundation stone for the *Johannes Bau* (Goetheanum) in Dornach. Building begins immediately. The third mystery drama, *The Soul's Awakening* (CW 14), is completed.

Also: *The Threshold of the Spiritual World* (CW 147). Lecture cycles include: *The Bhagavad Gita and the Epistles of Paul* and *The Esoteric Meaning of the Bhagavad Gita* (CW 146), which the Russian philosopher Nikolai Berdyaev attends; *The Mysteries of the East and of Christianity* (CW 144); *The Effects of Esoteric Development* (CW 145); and *The Fifth Gospel* (CW 148). In May, Rudolf Steiner is in London and Paris, where anthroposophical work continues.

1914: Building continues on the *Johannes Bau* (Goetheanum) in Dornach, with artists and coworkers from seventeen nations. The general assembly of the Anthroposophical Society takes place. In May, Rudolf Steiner visits Paris, as well as Chartres Cathedral. June 28: assassination in Sarajevo ("Now the catastrophe has happened!"). August 1: War is declared. Rudolf Steiner returns to Germany from Dornach—he will travel back and forth. He writes the last chapter of *The Riddles of Philosophy*. Lecture cycles include: *Human and Cosmic Thought* (CW 151); *Inner Being of Humanity between Death and a New Birth* (CW 153); *Occult Reading and Occult Hearing* (CW 156). December 24: marriage of Rudolf Steiner and Marie von Sivers.

1915: Building continues. Life after death becomes a major theme, also art. Writes: *Thoughts during a Time of War* (CW 24). Lectures include: *The Secret of Death* (CW 159); *The Uniting of Humanity through the Christ Impulse* (CW 165).

1916: Rudolf Steiner begins work with Edith Maryon (1872-1924) on the sculpture "The Representative of Humanity" ("The Group"—Christ, Lucifer, and Ahriman). He also works with the alchemist Alexander von Bernus on the quarterly *Das Reich*. He writes *The Riddle of Humanity* (CW 20). Lectures include: *Necessity and Freedom in World History and Human Action* (CW 166); *Past and Present in the Human Spirit* (CW 167); *The Karma of Vocation* (CW 172); *The Karma of Untruthfulness* (CW 173).

1917: Russian Revolution. The U.S. enters the war. Building continues. Rudolf Steiner delineates the idea of the "threefold nature of the human being" (in a public lecture March 15) and the "threefold nature of the social organism" (hammered out in May-June with the help of Otto von Lerchenfeld and Ludwig Polzer-Hoditz in the form of two documents titled *Memoranda*, which were distributed in high places). August-September: Rudolf Steiner writes *The Riddles of the Soul* (CW 20). Also: commentary on "The Chemical Wedding of Christian Rosenkreutz" for Alexander Bernus (*Das Reich*). Lectures include: *The Karma of Materialism* (CW 176); *The Spiritual Background of the Outer World: The Fall of the Spirits of Darkness* (CW 177).

1918: March 18: peace treaty of Brest-Litovsk—"Now everything will truly enter chaos! What is needed is cultural renewal." June: Rudolf Steiner visits Karlstein (Grail) Castle outside Prague. Lecture cycle: *From Symptom to Reality in Modern History* (CW 185). In mid-November,

Emil Molt, of the Waldorf-Astoria Cigarette Company, has the idea of founding a school for his workers' children.

1919: Focus on the threefold social organism: tireless travel, countless lectures, meetings, and publications. At the same time, a new public stage of Anthroposophy emerges as cultural renewal begins. The coming years will see initiatives in pedagogy, medicine, pharmacology, and agriculture. January 27: threefold meeting: " We must first of all, with the money we have, found free schools that can bring people what they need." February: first public eurythmy performance in Zurich. Also: "Appeal to the German People" (CW 24), circulated March 6 as a newspaper insert. In April, *Toward Social Renewal* (CW 23)—"perhaps the most widely read of all books on politics appearing since the war"—appears. Rudolf Steiner is asked to undertake the "direction and leadership" of the school founded by the Waldorf-Astoria Company. Rudolf Steiner begins to talk about the "renewal" of education. May 30: a building is selected and purchased for the future Waldorf School. August-September, Rudolf Steiner gives a lecture course for Waldorf teachers, *The Foundations of Human Experience (Study of Man)* (CW 293). September 7: Opening of the first Waldorf School. December (into January): first science course, the *Light Course* (CW 320).

1920: The Waldorf School flourishes. New threefold initiatives. Founding of limited companies *Der Kommenden Tag* and *Futurum A.G.* to infuse spiritual values into the economic realm. Rudolf Steiner also focuses on the sciences. Lectures: *Introducing Anthroposophical Medicine* (CW 312); *The Warmth Course* (CW 321); *The Boundaries of Natural Science* (CW 322); *The Redemption of Thinking* (CW 74). February: Johannes Werner Klein—later a cofounder of the Christian Community—asks Rudolf Steiner about the possibility of a "religious renewal," a "Johannine church." In March, Rudolf Steiner gives the first course for doctors and medical students. In April, a divinity student asks Rudolf Steiner a second time about the possibility of religious renewal. September 27-October 16: anthroposophical "university course." December: lectures titled *The Search for the New Isis* (CW 202).

1921: Rudolf Steiner continues his intensive work on cultural renewal, including the uphill battle for the threefold social order. "University" arts, scientific, theological, and medical courses include: *The Astronomy Course* (CW 323); *Observation, Mathematics, and Scientific Experiment* (CW 324); the *Second Medical Course* (CW 313); *Color.* In June and September-October, Rudolf Steiner also gives the first two "priests' courses" (CW 342 and 343). The "youth movement" gains momentum. Magazines are founded: *Die Drei* (January), and—under the editorship of Albert Steffen (1884-1963)—the weekly, *Das Goetheanum* (August). In February-March, Rudolf Steiner takes his first trip outside Germany since the war (Holland). On April 7, Steiner receives a letter regarding "religious renewal," and May 22-23, he agrees to address the question in a practical way. In June, the Klinical-Therapeutic Institute opens in Arlesheim under the direction of Dr. Ita Wegman. In August, the Chemical-Pharmaceutical Laboratory opens in Arlesheim (Oskar Schmiedel and Ita Wegman, directors). The Clinical Therapeutic Institute is inaugurated in Stuttgart (Dr. Ludwig Noll, director); also the Research Laboratory in Dornach (Ehrenfried Pfeiffer and Gunther Wachsmuth, directors). In November-December, Rudolf Steiner visits Norway.

1922: The first half of the year involves very active public lecturing (thousands attend); in the second half, Rudolf Steiner begins to withdraw and turn toward the Society—"The Society is asleep." It is "too weak" to do what is asked of it. The businesses—*Die Kommenden Tag* and *Futura A.G.*—fail. In January, with the help of an agent, Steiner undertakes a twelve-city German tour, accompanied by eurythmy performances. In two weeks he speaks to more than 2,000 people. In April, he gives a "university course" in The Hague. He also visits England. In June, he is in Vienna for the East-West Congress. In August-September, he is back in England for the Oxford Conference on Education. Returning to Dornach, he gives the lectures *Philosophy, Cosmology, and Religion* (CW 215), and gives the third priest's course (CW 344). On September 16, The Christian Community is founded. In October-November, Steiner is in Holland and England. He also speaks to the youth: *The Youth Course* (CW 217). In December, Steiner gives lectures titled *The Origins of Natural Science* (CW 326), and *Humanity and the World of Stars: The Spiritual Communion of Humanity* (CW 219). December 31: Fire at the Goetheanum, which is destroyed.

1923: Despite the fire, Rudolf Steiner continues his work unabated. A very hard year. Internal dispersion, dissension, and apathy abound. There is conflict—between old and new visions—within the society. A wake-up call is needed, and Rudolf Steiner responds with renewed lecturing vitality. His focus: the spiritual context of human life; initiation science; the course of the year; and community building. As a foundation for an artistic school, he creates a series of pastel sketches. Lecture cycles: *The Anthroposophical Movement; Initiation Science* (CW 227) (in England at the Penmaenmawr Summer School); *The Four Seasons and the Archangels* (CW 229); *Harmony of the Creative Word* (CW 230); *The Supersensible Human* (CW 231), given in Holland for the founding of the Dutch society. On November 10, in response to the failed Hitler-Ludendorf putsch in Munich, Steiner closes his Berlin residence and moves the *Philosophisch-Anthroposophisch Verlag* (Press) to Dornach. On December 9, Steiner begins the serialization of his *Autobiography: The Course of My Life* (CW 28) in *Das Goetheanum.* It will continue to appear weekly, without a break, until his death. Late December-early January: Rudolf Steiner refounds the Anthroposophical Society (about 12,000 members internationally) and takes over its leadership. The new board members are: Marie Steiner, Ita Wegman, Albert Steffen, Elizabeth Vreede, and Guenther Wachsmuth. (See *The Christmas Meeting for the Founding of the General Anthroposophical Society* (CW 260). Accompanying lectures: *Mystery Knowledge and Mystery Centers* (CW 232); *World History in the Light of Anthroposophy* (CW 233). December 25: the Foundation Stone is laid (in the hearts of members) in the form of the "Foundation Stone Meditation."

1924: January 1: having founded the Anthroposophical Society and taken over its leadership, Rudolf Steiner has the task of "reforming" it. The process begins with a weekly newssheet ("What's Happening in the Anthroposophical Society") in which Rudolf Steiner's "Letters to Members" and "Anthroposophical Leading Thoughts" appear (CW 26). The next step is the creation of a new esoteric class, the "first class" of the "University of Spiritual Science" (which was to have been followed, had Rudolf Steiner lived longer, by two more advanced classes). Then comes a new language for Anthroposophy—practical, phenomenological, and direct; and Rudolf Steiner creates the model for the second Goetheanum. He begins the series of extensive "karma" lectures (CW 235-40); and finally, responding to needs, he creates two new initiatives: biodynamic agriculture and curative education. After the middle of the year, rumors begin to circulate regarding Steiner's health. Lectures: January-February, *Anthroposophy* (CW 234); February: *Tone Eurythmy* (CW 278); June: *The Agriculture Course* (CW 327); June-July: Speech [?] Eurythmy (CW 279); *Curative Education* (CW 317); August: (England, "Second International Summer School"), *Initiation Consciousness: True and False Paths in Spiritual Investigation* (CW 243); September: *Pastoral Medicine* (CW 318). On September 26, for the first time, Rudolf Steiner cancels a lecture. On September 28, he gives his last lecture. On September 29, he withdraws to his studio in the carpenter's shop; now he is definitively ill. Cared for by Ita Wegman, he continues working, however, and writing the weekly installments of his *Autobiography* and *Letters to the Members/Leading Thoughts* (CW 26).

1925: Rudolf Steiner, while continuing to work, continues to weaken. He finishes *Extending Practical Medicine* (CW 27) with Ita Wegman. On March 30, around ten in the morning, Rudolf Steiner dies.

# INDEX